BLACK LIGHT

Perspectives on Mysterious Phenomena

William J. Grabowski

▲

Oblivion Press
2014

BLACK LIGHT: Perspectives on Mysterious Phenomena
Copyright © 2014 by William J. Grabowski

Cover design © 2014 by William J. Grabowski

This print edition © 2014 Oblivion Press
All rights reserved.

ISBN: 097496283X
ISBN-13: 978-0974962832

"Broken Symmetry"
Copyright © 2014 by William J. Grabowski

"Telegram from a Cold War Kid: An Interview with William J. Grabowski"
Copyright © 2014 by Lee Munro

Contact: nightrun7@yahoo.com

Any Internet references contained in this work are current at publication time, but the publisher cannot guarantee that a specific location will continue to be maintained.

ACKNOWLEDGMENTS

A book such as this, while written under solitary conditions, isn't researched that way. I did my best to leave others alone, much as I prefer, but no book—especially nonfiction—is conceived and written in perfect vacuum. I'm grateful for the help of a few whose work and integrity are to me unassailable. They are: Jack Brewer, Doug Skinner, Lee Munro, John Rimmer, George P. Hansen, Director Mark Pellington, George Knapp of KLAS-TV, Martin Kottmeyer, Andy Colvin, Jeff Wamsley, Aaron last-name-unknown of WCHS-TV, who interviewed me in Point Pleasant, WV, and apparently was subdued by the MIB (the interview was never broadcast!), Stan Gordon, Jacques Vallee, the venerable Thornton M. Vaseltarp—literary agent (who claims to know more than I about John A. Keel), Tim and Beth Walker, Alan Sparhawk and Mimi Parker of Duluth band Low, Michael J. Nelson (he of *Mystery Science Theater 3000* and RiffTrax), the inexplicable Tom Waits, *that* Bruce Campbell, *Fortean Times*, uni-ball® Vision™ felt-tip pens, all hot pepper products, coffee, and Yuengling Beer.

W.J.G.

CONTENTS

"Any form of collective thought is subject to influence and suggestion, and blind on fundamentals. Free individual thought, the reflective work of a solitary researcher, is the best path to discovery. It is subject to mistakes but those are easier to correct, provided one stays close to key facts and seeks the advice of independent thinkers. That ingredient—critical thought—is the most difficult one to find."

—Jacques Vallee
Forbidden Science, Vol. Two

INTRODUCTION

I approached this project with more than a little trepidation. Does the world need yet another book about so-called paranormal phenomena? I asked myself. If so, am I qualified to write it? The great visionary poet William Blake wrote that the road of excess leads to the palace of wisdom. Let us hope. All pretense aside, what I mean by quoting Blake is that I have read hundreds of volumes—ancient to modern—devoted to events uncanny, anomalous, and—occasionally—terrifying. Many of these are ludicrous and poorly written. Some I flung against the nearest wall, cursing myself for wasting hard-won dollars. The Internet offers mountains of pages, many (but not all) as spurious as printed matter.

Nowhere, excepting politics, religion, and Wall Street, will one encounter as many charlatans, liars, hoaxers and outright loonies as prevail in affairs paranormal. A harsh truth, but there it is. The most important studies—out of hundreds—number fewer than 50, many of these culled from one another.

Reading books does not make one an authority (or Authority!), whatever the topic. Scrutinizing 10,000 cookbooks, without hands-on experience, will not enable one to prepare a Thai delicacy.

During the final editing of this book, I gathered every scrap I had piled up since the mid-1980s, when my first "paranormal" articles were published (alongside those of Stan Gordon, he of Kecksburg UFO-crash infamy) in Beth Robbins' *The Gate*. A huge pile of crap (my "notes," not Beth's magazine). I could not have known that, 13 years hence, I'd be residing in Pennsylvania several miles from Gordon and 25 minutes by car to Kecksburg, and on the wrong end of a telephone trying to convince Stan that sightings of black triangular UFOs were generated by terrestrial assets. For the record, we agreed to disagree. Stan remains one of the hardest-working investigators (meaning he mans a 24/7 hotline and ventures out under all conditions—no easy task in southwest Pennsylvania).

My unpublished, mostly beer-fueled scribbles, recorded once in a while after all-night observing sessions with friends and their various telescopes, remain shockingly crude—a necessary passage through personal belief and fear. Because these ideas felt emotionally "right," I was attracted to the Extraterrestrial Hypothesis, something now impossible for me to take seriously, though one I cannot rule out. In our current ever-credulous society,

I'd sooner try and disprove the existence of God.

Attentive readers will realize *Black Light* has more in common with sociological studies of folklore than with ufology and parapsychology—I covet the wine, not the bottle. John Keel considered his investigations into "folklore in the making" as noteworthy; he was not, ultimately, alone in this assessment. I wish readers to consider the present book an artifact retrieved from the unknown by an explorer of existence. *A reflection on the source of whatever hidden—intentionally or not; external or not—mechanism or process triggers our capacity for perceiving anomalous (often shattering) experiences.*

I have visited a scattering of haunted places; met the locals, broke their bread, and listened to accounts fascinating, comical, and ominous. We are a cynical, yet hopeful lot, with no idea what we are, where we came from, or why we're here. It's a universal fact that people are more haunted than any landscape, house, or patch of sky. No mystery: we share a world vibrant with wonder, horror, and uncertainty, where (as poignantly noted by author William Gibson) "We have no future because our present is too volatile. We have only risk management..."

Let's face it: nobody gets out of here alive. Except, apparently, on a few very rare occasions.

Like these lonely travelers, I have had several strange encounters that haunt me still. Frankly, I wish they didn't. These evoke unpleasant possibilities that might have nothing whatsoever to do with the "paranormal." Sharper, braver souls than me have noted that sometimes the "explanation" for anomalous events can be weirder far than the events themselves.

I cannot claim final knowledge of what I did, or did not, experience. But the memories—if genuine—charge me with an undeniable sense that *something is here, something other than us.* What that might be I cannot say, but am prepared to accept the high probability it is a projection of humanity's awful loneliness, and growing spiritual despair. The poet Arthur Rimbaud remarked that he desired to total the sum of the unknown. A lofty goal indeed, for the unknown takes many forms, strips away all defense and comfort; forces us to confront (as noted by Carl Jung) a psychically overwhelming Other—for good or ill.

The paranormal (including authentic unexplained UFOs), whatever it might represent, is something no government, institution, or individual can conceal or control.

The late, much-lamented, John A. Keel (author of *The Mothman Prophecies, The Eighth Tower, Operation Trojan Horse* and others) noted that most books on topics paranormal sell fewer than several thousand copies. With apologies to Mr. Keel, I'm reasonably sure I can point out a few—some penned by Keel himself—that fared better. Why this sorry state of affairs exists, I have no idea. Perhaps the absurdity of the subject matter; perhaps its dire, disturbing implications. We live in a grim place, with no indication of better things on the horizon.

The field of paranormal study, like some dysfunctional family, is combative, lurid, and incestuous. Rife with vapid drama and petty sniping sufficient to render afternoon soap operas dignified. So it has ever been....

Those who ignore, or falsify, the data are making a serious mistake.

Fact: UFOs and other paranormal manifestations exist. What they might actually be is another question. Governments worldwide know this. Whether they still care is another relevant question. The post-World War II UFO sightings were taken quite seriously as conceivable threats to national security. Several studies throughout the 1940s (Project Sign, 1947; Project Grudge, 1949), 1950s (the Central Intelligence Agency's Robertson Panel, formed after the July 1952 radar and visual UFO sightings—allegedly involving 2008 presidential nominee John McCain—near the National Airport in Washington, D.C), and 1960s, notably the United States Air Force's 1968 Condon Report dismissed the phenomenon, which guaranteed genuine scientists would ignore it. Jacques Vallee referred to the Condon affair as "that fine piece of scientific recklessness." The often-cited Project Blue Book (1952-1970), which collected a huge database, while under Major Hector Quintanilla's tenure, had project consultant J. Allen Hynek remarking: "The flag of the utter nonsense school was flying at its highest on the mast."

Fact: no government knows what these things are, where they originate, or their intent—if any.

From the outset I determined to be as fair and objective as possible reporting any involvement global intelligence agencies might have with the manifold phenomena. Since there is no way to measure this, I can only hope that members of (un)said agencies have as part of their goals our best interests. Despite the swarm of conspiracy theories (many of which are ill-informed, unlikely, and —disturbingly—cut-outs for various hate-groups, or simply crazy), those entrusted with our protection are—believe it or not—human beings. Pissed-off by the alarm clock, struggling from bed, feeding their children and driving to work.

Are there bad players among them? Of course; try and find *any* organization without these. Beyond what you've seen on *The X-Files* and similar fare, there is but one genuine "conspiracy": government awareness of anomalous phenomena, and that official authority is powerless against this. A simple reality for thousands of years, and unlikely ever to change. Ancient Rome was as troubled by "poltergeists," zigzaggy nocturnal lights, and foggy apparitions as any present-day "window area" or local cold-zone.

Fact: no government can, or will, admit to such impotence.

Perhaps this explains the disinformation, staged events, lies, and outright threats. After all, those in charge are as vulnerable to hope and fear as any of us.

One thing I can promise is that I have no personal or professional agenda, no ax to grind, in writing this book. I come to you not as a scientist, researcher, or zealot; but as a writer. In short, from a fascination with what appears to be an authentic unknown among us.

From all accounts, we are faced with what appears to be an absolute, yet ever-evolving, aspect of existence that might forever remain unsolvable. It can be dangerous; even lethal. It has changed for the better as many lives as it has ruined. We might be in the clutches either of something outside human comprehension, or—

despite our collective craving and spiritual despair—even incidental to our lives. Like a fish hooked out of water, we might very well be incapable of understanding what we have no model for.

The only thing worse than this would be abandoning the search for illumination, whatever that might reveal....

Though my quest might be ultimately foolish, it is sincere. Perhaps "God" (Goddess?) really is in the details.

Unlike *The X-Files'* Fox Mulder, I don't want to believe.

I want to understand.

—William J. Grabowski

"We're not here to capture an image, we're here to maintain one. Every photograph reinforces the aura. Can you feel it, Jack? An accumulation of nameless energies."

—Murray Jay Siskind
in Don DeLillo's *White Noise*

1. COLD WAR KID

In the northeast Ohio summer of 1968, a 10-year-old boy saw a strange thing.

The day was hot and the boy anticipated jumping into the small above-ground swimming pool assembled by his father. Stepping across the warm lawn toward the plywood shed (also built by Father), the boy noticed something scurrying behind the red structure.

What the heck is that?

He paused, moved stealthily ahead, clover brushing his bare feet. Peeking around the shed's corner, he gasped. Not 10 feet away stood a funny-looking bird—or something.

It might have been two- or three-feet tall, liquid black eyes and pointed beak gleaming in the sun.

Shocked, the boy backed away. *Is that a penguin?*

It sure resembled one, but something about the way it glared at him felt wrong. Not to mention a queasy fear evoked by the gray, plump form and wings tucked tight against this. The unnatural stillness.

Abruptly the thing waddled toward the boy—he cried out, turned and dashed toward the house. *What is it what is it what is it?!*

What it might be he didn't know, but it scared the hell out of him. Why did it exist? What did it want?

In a swirl of fright the boy burst into the house and up the stairs into the kitchen, where stood his mother washing dishes from lunch. "My god," she said, "what happened to you? You're white as a sheet!"

Though he fought against it, the boy suddenly wept, clamped his arms around Mother. "I saw—I saw a monster behind the shed..."

"What?"

The boy cried and cried. "Go see, go see—please."

"Oh brother, let's go."

The boy shook his head. "No! Don't make me go back. I *can't*. It's not allowed."

"Not allowed? Settle down. Have a glass of water and I'll take a look."

After several minutes, she returned. "There's nothing out there, honey. Tell me what you saw."

The boy gulped water as if he hadn't had any for days. Glass after glass, to the point of nausea. His thirst wouldn't quit.

Later, after telling his mother (and father, home now from work in Cleveland) about the bizarre creature, the boy needed comfort. Though highly imaginative, he wasn't a liar or a trickster, and his parents knew this.

"C'mon," Dad said, "let's go downstairs and shine those new boots of yours."

"Okay...that sounds good."In the basement beside Dad's ordered workshop the two set up a home-made shoe-polishing box. Dad took a round tin of Kiwi-brand boot polish from the rig, and the boy paled. "That's it! That's what I saw."

Dad squinted with confusion. "This? The polish? What are you talking about?"

"No. The bird on the lid. It looked like *that*—but standing up..."

Dad grinned, glanced at the fat figure on the lid and its cartoon-like form. "You couldn't have seen that here. Not in Ohio."

"But I *did*!"

"No. Kiwis don't live in the northern hemisphere. I learned that in school."

And there the matter ended. Or did it?

The boy could not have known that, between 1966 and 1969, a UFO "wave" was besieging America. In fact, children in Holmes County [1] had reported seeing a silver, saucer-shaped craft hovering near where they were playing. Nor could the boy have been aware that people in Beaver Falls (75 miles southeast), Pennsylvania, had run into a number of very strange "birds," reported to be nearly eight-feet tall, plump, with straight pointed beaks. These witnesses watched the incredible entities scatter through a cornfield and into trees. A man's hunting dog, unleashed, fled yelping in terror.

Forty-four years later, our no-longer-young witness read of a UFO being chased by police in April 1966 from Ravenna [2] (a half-hour drive from his boyhood home) into Pennsylvania, where it vanished. One of these policemen had his life ruined by the event, and took refuge in the Solon Motel—one mile from the boy's home. This was proof of UFO activity in the area, although possibly unconnected to the "entity" sighting.

Another thing unknown to him was that almost two years before his frightening encounter, over 100 people in and around the quiet Ohio Valley town of Point Pleasant, West Virginia [3], reported sightings of "Mothman," an eight-foot-tall entity with bat-like wings and terrible red-glowing eyes. Too, the boy (as well as most UFO/paranormal investigators of the time) knew nothing of the phenomenon called "screen memory," where a witness to some traumatic event fantasizes he saw something other than what actually occurred, in order to cope with overwhelming anxiety and fear.

The boy's frightening, incomprehensible experience sparked in him a life-long fascination with so-called paranormal phenomena. In the decades to follow, he had several more mysterious encounters with the unknown. These he shared with no one until much later in life.

He matured to become a somewhat troubled, if not troublesome, man haunted by these enigmas.

I know this case intimately, because the man is me.

NOTES:

1. VALLEE, Jacques. *Passport to Magonia: On UFOs, Folklore, and Parallel Worlds* (Contemporary Books, 1969; 1993).

2. KEEL, John A. *The Eighth Tower: On Ultraterrestrials and the Superspectrum* (New York; *Saturday Review Press*, 1975; 2013 Anomalist Books edition).

3. KEEL, John A. *The Mothman Prophecies* (New York; *Saturday Review Press*, 1975; 2002 Tor Edition).

2. BELIEF IS THE ENEMY

A seemingly impossible-to-breach barrier awaits any serious explorer of mysterious phenomena: belief systems.

It is difficult indeed to underestimate the practically suffocating power of belief, for it is made of emotion. Those who investigate ghosts, poltergeist activity, "channeling," and the spectrum of psychic phenomena, often ignore or ridicule the field of UFO studies—and vice versa. This tension functions like a class-system, with each investigator specializing in a particular area and often considering himself superior to those working elsewhere. Each find it very hard to accept that all anomalous events are connected. This is what Charles Fort [1] hinted when he wrote that a circle can be measured by starting anywhere, and when he noted the "underlying oneness in all confusions" (which may as well stand as an alternate—if clumsy—subtitle for this book).

Even Fort's present-day critics must admit his perspectives were —and in many ways are still—decades ahead of their time (Fort's final book, *Wild Talents*, was published in 1932). Such belief-tainted subjectivity is at very least non-productive, and often as ugly as racism. No serious, or amateur, investigator should so behave. Anyone questioning this simply hasn't taken a long look at the voluminous—to say the least!—data. Worse, Fort's notion, now fact, of connectedness (despite its quantum "reality") only amplifies the disturbing effect of the phenomena themselves.

But there is another, more potent, factor against belief: the manifestations adjust their activities and forms in accordance with the local cultural-religious matrix—hence the danger.

Example: suppose I am an investigator, and a devout Roman Catholic. I am called to study a "haunting" in a nearby home, where I encounter elements of hostility in the "ghost." My religious beliefs more than likely will urge me to conclude the apparition is "evil." In fairness, I'll admit many people (even some atheists), when confronted by aggressive paranormal events, might perceive the source as evil. Such is the power of fright.

Similarly, if I believe UFOs are extraterrestrial and piloted by "Grays," I might suppress and/or ignore evidence pointing elsewhere. This enormous problem has tainted paranormal investigation since its inception. Please understand this is not an attack on the value of religious faith, though such ought not bias serious research.

Though True Believers hate hearing as much, there are a considerable number of absurd factors resident in many UFO reports. So absurd, the accounts evoke a dream-like, strangely poetic air. Then we have encounters that scream in terror, traumatize witnesses, and cause ruin.

As noted by the late Jim Keith (author of *Black Helicopters Over America, Casebook On the Men in Black* and many others), one's chronic emotional state seems to dictate the tone and texture of UFO/paranormal experiences. This suggests, to an extent, that we project both conscious and subconscious content onto anomalous events, perhaps as a coping mechanism, or simply as a form of pattern-recognition. There is, however, an external trigger; though what follows is colored by the individual's cultural milieu and/or belief system. Jacques Vallee and John Keel arrived at this conclusion in the 1960s, and I've not encountered any other theories worth taking seriously. Note that I consider this a thick branch of the so-called psychosocial hypothesis formed in the early 1980s by Hilary Evans [2], Bertrand Méheust, Thierry Pinvidic, and a few others.

Another, albeit little-examined, aspect of beliefs and their origin is media-driven.

I make no great claim to be authoritative on media-treatment of the paranormal, but I do pay attention. Even a cursory glance at cinema and television over the past few years tells anyone with a pulse that the only subject as exploited as sex and death is the paranormal which, sadly, generates more bullshit than Wall Street. If I didn't know better, and sometimes I'm sure I don't, I'd say the American people are a gullible lot. On the other hand, what are we to do? Boycotting movies won't change anything and, frankly, strikes me as hysterical and censorious. There *is* a lack of discretion, and this bothers me.

Granted, few of us have time even to consider our viewing-options. I admit to enjoying—very much—some visual junk-food, especially *Mystery Science Theater 3000* [3]. But I understand the difference between that and genuine nourishment. (Then again, isn't something that erases neurotic gloom genuine nourishment?)

No, this does not make me morally superior; simply better informed. I expect more from my entertainment, knowing as well that occasionally there's nothing as satisfying as General Tso's Chicken or a bag of Fritos. This makes my next observation all the more difficult.

Cinematic special-effects have advanced to a degree of nearly unparalleled realism. Or illusion; your call. We have, on TV, *CSI*, *Person of Interest*, etc., and their legion of imitators. James Cameron's *Avatar* raised the stakes yet higher (too bad he wasn't involved in raising anything on *Terminator* sequels after the second film). The prevalence of ever-evolving computer wizardry is clearly visible in science fiction, horror, fantasy, and even mainstream media. But visuals are visuals—nothing more. The underlying structure, storytelling, has not advanced at the same manic pace.

Similarly, stating the all-too-obvious, human ethics have failed to keep up with scientific and military progress (where daily news feeds show us, in the guise of UAVs—drones—a Faustian marriage of media and science).

For what it's worth, I will mention two fairly strong—and one outstanding—examples of paranormality in film: *Paranormal Activity* (2009) [4], and *The Fourth Kind* (2009) [5]. I fully realize the perils of comparing films to books, but these are thoughtful, (mostly) intelligent works. I am aware that *The Fourth Kind* misrepresented itself as based on "true" events, and fail to see why its makers thought this necessary. Perhaps they were forced. Though I have viewed, and been disappointed by, the *Paranormal Activity* sequels, this does not rob the original of its raw power. As a writer of (fictional) horror, I know that such work will fail if not invested with emotional and psychological realism. Both *PA* and *TFK* manage this realism admirably. Here is film-making composed with minimal effects, i.e. CGI and its ilk, and focusing on the human aspects. And what aspects!

While fine (if not exactly restrained) examples, these offerings are clearly overshadowed by director Mark Pellington's intensely creepy and emotional *The Mothman Prophecies* (2002) [6]. I cannot imagine a more perfectly suited artist to handle the difficult adaptation of John A. Keel's 1975 nonfiction book. Pellington's every shot bleeds humanity, sadness, dread, and a throbbing paranoia (aided by "noise-meister" Glenn Branca, Tomandandy, and King Black Acid) that literally vibrates nerves.

Say what you will, but these films more than likely scared you and engaged your mind—no small accomplishment. This proves it is possible to produce material for mass consumption that is intelligent and entertaining, when the producers actually give a damn.

My reason for even the briefest mention of cinema is this: it is safe to say that most people's awareness of UFO/paranormal matters derives from movies and TV—a mixed bag indeed. Sadly, most (but not all, i.e., *The Mothman Prophecies*) of this material seriously misrepresents the extant data for mere thrills and

10

exploitation. In short, "dumbing down" the stuff in order to render it—like baby food—palatable.

We deserve better.

NOTES:

1. FORT, Charles. *The Book of the Damned* (first published 1919; Jeremy P. Tarcher/Penguin collected edition 2008). *New Lands* (1923; Jeremy P. Tarcher/Penguin collected edition 2008). *Lo!* (1931; Jeremy P. Tarcher/Penguin collected edition 2008). *Wild Talents* (1932; Jeremy P. Tarcher/Penguin collected edition 2008).
2. http://pelicanist.blogspot.com/2011/07/remembering-hilary.html
3. http://www.mst3k.com/
4. *Paranormal Activity* (Blumhouse Productions; 2009).
5. *The Fourth Kind* (Gold Circle Films; 2009).
6. *The Mothman Prophecies* (Lakeshore Entertainment; 2002).

3. MOTHMAN REDUX

I think it's a fair assumption that most readers of UFO/paranormal literature are familiar—perhaps overly so—with the events that occurred between 1966-1968 (in fact sightings of UFOs and entities were reported before and after these dates, so consider this simply the period of highest activity) at Point Pleasant, West Virginia, and nearby. Mothman [1]; "thunderbirds"; UFOs and their apparent occupants; Men in Black menacing locals; poltergeist outbreaks; eerie synchronicities, and literally the spectrum of psychic phenomena.

I am not aware of any other single location having been besieged by so much for so long.

This chapter, though based on extant material, will not be a simple rehash. While I cannot claim to have reviewed all published (and filmed) material, I am confident that I've come close, since much cross-over exists in the data. Too, I have visited Point Pleasant a number of times, conversed with many residents (including some who witnessed UFO and/or paranormal occurrences), and explored much of the area covered in this book.

For those unfamiliar with the events, a recitation of the most well-known incident is called for. On Tuesday, 15 November 1966, around 11:00PM, two teenaged couples, Roger and Linda Scarberry, Steve and Mary Mallette, were riding in Roger's 1957

Chevy through the so-called TNT Area some seven miles north of Point Pleasant. (Also known as the West Virginia Ordnance Works, the vast landscape served during World War Two as a munitions plant, employing thousands. Today, after considerable reclamation, it is called McClintic Wildlife Management Area.) The night was clear and cold. Nearing the old North power plant, the car's headlights illuminated two red circles roughly two inches in diameter. Whatever it was stood near the old power-house (since demolished), and apparently took wing, pursuing the car at speeds approaching 100 miles-per-hour. Even today, I cannot imagine anyone driving so fast on Route 62. Though flat, parallel to the Ohio River, the road has several curves and in utter darkness is treacherous. It remains unlighted. You wouldn't want to drive any faster than the (posted) 40 mph.

This was no joke. The couples headed directly for the police station on Main Street, and gave a statement. None of them had any history as troublemakers—quite the opposite. During their terrifying experience, they noticed a dead dog on the roadside. What they didn't know was that the previous night a man living near Salem, WV, had set his dog upon some dark figure with fiery red eyes. Newell Partridge never saw his trusty German shepherd —Bandit—again.

Later, accompanied by Point Pleasant Deputy Halstead, the couples drove back the 7 miles to the TNT [2] area. Notably absent was the dead dog. While much has been made of this, it is possible that the dog was not dead, though injured, and simply managed to wander off. We'll never know, but the fact that it was noticed at all is important.

Mothman, as described by the witnesses, could not possibly fly with its 10-foot-wide wingspan. As noted by John Keel, a creature of such size would require wings at least 30 feet wide to go airborne.

Which brings us to the matter at hand.

Hard as it might be to comprehend, the so-called Mothman entity remains the most difficult aspect to "explain." Everything else: UFOs, Men in Black, bizarre telephone intrusions, poltergeist activity, can be conceivably figured. This is why I think the entity itself was a genuine unknown.

I have studied in the open literature the capabilities of 1960s-era American intelligence agencies, and a number of aspects seem to resonate with at least some of the Point Pleasant events.

1. Only recently [3] has it been determined that the architects of the TNT Area outside Point Pleasant were the same who designed both the Manhattan Project (atom bomb) and Area-51. Though Area-51, if we can rely on the extant data, began in 1952, this places both the Manhattan Project and the TNT Area as simultaneous works.

2. I realize that any TNT activity had to be secret. One can go on a tour and visit 100 "igloos" (concrete domes covered with earth and fitted with bomb-proof hatches) built on a staggered grid to prevent both aerial detection and complete ruin from air-strike. These structures still exist.

3. The genesis of the TNT Area is suspicious, given post-WWII anomalous activity. "Animal experimentation" took place there. Why? Certainly, even between 1942-1945 (when TNT was alive), no one would have been lining up livestock on the firing-range. So what could have necessitated their presence?

4. Some of the 100 igloos were later leased to Mason County government. Others were sold to the Trojan-U.S. Powder Co. and the LFC Chemical concern. A few were leased to American Cyanamid. From Nick Redfern's and Andy Robert's *Strange Secrets: Real Government Files on the Unknown* [4]: "During the summer of 1947, the FBI also interviewed one Edwin M. Bailey of Stamford, CT., who had concerns about man-made saucers and their use against the United States by an offensive nation. Bailey's comments were the subject of a memorandum to FBI Director [J. Edgar] Hoover.

"'Bailey prefaced his remarks by stating that he is a scientist by occupation and is currently employed at the American Cyanamid Research Laboratories...in Stamford, CT., in the Physics Division. Bailey further stated that during the war he was employed at MIT, Cambridge, MA., in the Radiation Laboratory which laboratory is connected with the Manhattan Project....

"'Bailey stated that the topic of flying saucers had caused considerable comment and concern to the present day scientists and indicated that he himself had a personal theory concerning the flying saucers...

"'Bailey stated that it is quite possible that actually the flying saucers could be radio-controlled germ bombs or atom bombs which are circling the orbit of the earth and which could be controlled by radio and directed to land on any designated target at the specific desire of the agency or country operating the bombs.'"

Given the future events that took place in Point Pleasant, I find this information more than a little telling about possible (perhaps necessary) U.S. government operations.

These connections might be spurious—but I doubt it.

Though it is easier, and more fun, to take the so-called Mothman events at face-value, I think there exist enough data to at least suggest, if not confirm, human involvement in what began long before the "paranormal" chaos centered in Point Pleasant.

As many readers of UFO/paranormal literature know, the "right" questions have been asked (notably by John Keel, Jim Keith [5], Gray Barker [6] —with qualification, due to Jim Moseley's [7] admission that he and Barker orchestrated some hoaxes—and Loren Coleman [8]) regarding the possible role of U.S. intelligence agencies in the Point Pleasant activities. I cannot help but illuminate several dark zones in this material.

Since I do respect these tireless investigators (all now gone, save for Loren Coleman), and forgive a few of them their unwise decisions, I must note that I agree with a few other writers that Gray Barker had a big hand in the Mothman weirdness. Moseley has publicly admitted his role in the so-called Straith letter hoax (cooked up one drunk night in Barker's Clarksburg, WV home) used against George Adamski [9] (typed on State Department letterhead to give Adamski the idea that his UFO experiences were being taken seriously), but has not acknowledged having any involvement in the Point Pleasant matters.

I don't think he *was* involved, simply because he lived too far away at the time, and apparently wasn't a persistently enthusiastic hoaxer. Keel has stated he scoured his own telephone records after receiving strange calls in his New York City apartment, and that some of these were placed by Gray Barker. Too, there is evidence that Barker might have pranked others over the phone utilizing recordings of electronic effects. These matters aside, other questions remain.

Why, for instance, if black operations were present in the Point Pleasant/TNT Area, concerning radiation experiments, the design of the atomic bomb (an admittedly far-out notion), biological testing, and the additional possibility of the vast landscape being employed for development and even test-flights of man-made UFOs, did the town not experience prolific anomalous events until the 1960s?

1. If UFO-type craft were being designed in the TNT Area, perhaps, in the 1940s, they were too unstable to be flown over a populous region, and the project was relocated to the far more desolate deserts of Nevada and/or New Mexico. Although it is now known that Area 51 is so-named because that was the year of its creation, and this would rule it out for any involvement with the TNT area and whatever operations—beyond producing explosives and other ammunition—may have occurred there. However, now

that it is known the designers of the Manhattan Project are the same who put together the TNT area and, later, Area 51, I can only remark, "Make of that what you will." Another significant fact is that three air force bases—Wright Patterson, Lockbourne (since renamed Rickenbacker, complete with a restaurant), and the Oakdale base south of Pittsburgh, are located within 200 miles of Point Pleasant.

2. TNT Area was active from 1942-1945, and even if UFO-type craft (using Paper Clip scientists from Nazi Germany) were produced there, by the time they were ready the war effort was winding down. The Point Pleasant events occurred during the Cold War, when paranoia ran high that Russia or China might attack America with A-bombs.

At 54, I'm old enough to remember the "safety-drills" we underwent during my first 3 years in school. People were genuinely afraid. It's a documented (unclassified) fact that our military forces feared UFOs were products of Russian and/or Chinese technology. Keep this in mind when considering what might have happened at Roswell.

It was conjectured that these countries would unleash upon the U.S. a staged UFO "invasion," thus clogging all communication channels and leaving us vulnerable to conventional attack.

Contrasting these theories is another well-documented, if little-recognized, fact: most Roswell residents, after reading the famous newspaper account, did *not* believe the crash had anything to do with extraterrestrials. In somewhat chilling contrast, by the mid-

1960s many believed UFOs did not originate on Earth.

In fact, as early as 1952, a joint CIA/Battelle meeting suggested using the UFO phenomenon as "psychological warfare." This information comes from the ominous Pentacle Memorandum [10], unearthed by Jacques Vallee when he was going through J. Allen Hynek's [11] papers, and will be explored here at length in Chapter 15.

The time was right for the Point Pleasant events. So much evidence exists in favor of man-made UFOs (from Germany, Russia, China, Italy, and America), even as early as 1939, many sightings since need to be re-evaluated. I am not claiming that all UFOs are products of human technology, but certainly many must be. The explosive (literally) presence of unmanned aerial vehicles —popularly known as drones—has added a new level of confusion, and is bound only to get worse.

Lending additional credibility to government involvement in the Point Pleasant events of the 1960s, are these statements from John Keel and Jim Keith (Keith died suspiciously in 1999 after surgery from a minor knee injury): Keel, from *Fate* magazine, Sept. 2007: "I returned to Point Pleasant several times in 1967, learning more about the phenomenon with each trip. Several contactees (people who thought they had met the flying saucer occupants) had emerged and I was hypnotizing them and studying them carefully. I found these people had two levels of memory. The first level, the surface level, recalled under hypnosis a fascinating adventure, usually of being taken aboard a wonderful flying saucer. But the hidden level, which was difficult to get at and usually took several hypnotic sessions before it could be reached, rejected the false memory (confabulation) and painted a different picture. Most of these contactees had been transported to a van or house where they were subjected to brain-washing techniques and injected with an unknown substance. They were given a confabulation to remember and were released.

"But no matter how hard I tried I couldn't find out who was doing this. The whole contactee syndrome was a fraud, but the contactees were innocent victims. Why was anyone going to all the trouble to create these contactees? Many people in West Virginia told me of seeing strange, unmarked vans cruising the back roads at night."

Jim Keith pursues a similar line in his *Casebook on the Men in Black* (1997): "During the period of the Mothman encounters, black limousines prowled the Point Pleasant area, stopping at rural homes. Deeply tanned men proclaimed themselves to be 'census-takers' and showed an inordinate interest in the children of the households."

Seattle investigator/writer/editor and West Virginia native, Andrew Colvin [12], in his *The Mothman's Photographer* DVD (2004), claims to have undergone unusual tests given by parties unknown in his early years. From his account the testers were looking for children of high-intelligence.

Keith continues: "People in the rural areas also reported seeing mysterious unmarked panel trucks which parked in remote locations for hours, and were rumored to be Air Force. Men in coveralls worked on telephone and powerlines.

"A thirtyish blond woman visited people in Ohio and West Virginia, telling people she was John Keel's secretary, and filling out lengthy forms with information about health, income, family background, the types of cars the people owned, along with questions about UFO and Mothman sightings. Keel, naturally, did not have a secretary."

This suggests, if I may be so bold, the genesis of data-farming under the guise of the UFO/Paranormal phenomenon; something that, today, would not fly. We are not consumers of products. We *are* the product.

After all, we now have the Internet (conceived and created by American intelligence) to provide anyone who desires our most personal data.

Though many questions linger regarding the Point Pleasant events of 1966-1968, the one that most bothers me is why, given the undeniable amount of activity, these did not attract more outside attention.

Is this due to simple denial of unpleasant events, or to something else?

In a very real way, what happened there ruined (and ended, given the collapse of the Silver Bridge) many lives. This is beyond argument. While the official take on the bridge catastrophe (failure of the 13th eye-bar, a cracked metal disc on the Ohio-side) sounds correct, there might be more to it.

I have visited the Silver Bridge Memorial on the Ohio (and West Virginia) side, which features one of the eye-bars embedded in concrete. It is easy to see that, if even one failed, the entire bridge-span was gone. The Silver Bridge, constructed in the 1920s, was not in good shape. Locals described it as shaky, bobbing up and down (which, granted, many bridges do), and feared the structure was not equal to the newly heavy traffic of the 1960s.

Sadly, they were right. But the collapse instigated new safety inspection laws, a damned good idea.

Anyone well-versed in the entire matter will know that a woman on the Ohio side reported seeing two men climbing on the superstructure the day before the tragedy. These appeared to be men in thick-soled (oft-reported in Men-in-Black encounters) shoes. Even without the extremely cold weather, why would anyone actually climb along the bridge?

It's frankly suicidal, which doesn't mean I doubt the witness. Though I hate saying so, this seems to have happened in order to establish human sabotage. Why? The wreckage was reassembled in a field in nearby Henderson, WV, a process John Keel describes as brutally hard. It must have been, given that divers were brought in to search for bodies, and to assist enormous cranes necessary to raise the rubble.

Anyone curious about this bleak operation can see actual film footage shown at the Mothman Museum [13] in Point Pleasant. There isn't much, but what exists is haunting enough. The sort of thing—like 9/11—you might not want to see twice. A good deal of this footage is available on YouTube.

It is terrible, period, that the bridge came down. The context within which this happened makes it worse. This is why I give high marks to director Mark Pellington [14] whose 2002 film *The Mothman Prophecies* [15], despite numerous bitchy critics obviously unfamiliar with the source material, did manage to explore the chilling, incomprehensible Point Pleasant chaos with very human emotional authenticity. This aspect alone is almost unheard of in current cinematic treatments of the literature.

As someone who has driven, and walked, much of Point Pleasant and surrounding areas, I can claim there is a vast difference between reading about the events, and conversing and sharing meals with, people forever haunted by the phenomenon.

Some will not talk about it; some are hostile toward the annual Mothman Festival, yet in my experience most locals see the fest as a sort of catharsis, a way to discuss and share what might look to "outsiders" as crazy.

I'm not the first to notice how the horrible events have infused Point Pleasant with both much-needed commerce and an odd sense of community. No one attending the festival causes trouble or grief. The beauty of Jeff Wamsley's [16] and Carolin Harris's (Carolin owns the Harris Steak House on Main Street, and lost immediate family when the Silver Bridge collapsed) genesis of the fest is that they understand it as healing. The Mothman Festival takes place in mid-September.

What follows here owes its existence to the aforementioned

Andrew Colvin, self-proclaimed Mothman experiencer and gifted (or cursed) film-maker. I'd vote on the gifted-side, since Andy has worked with the likes of Laurie Anderson, several people associated with Andy Warhol's "factory," and even with Dennis Hopper on *Texas Chainsaw Massacre II.* And many more I hope Andy won't mind me not mentioning in this limited space.

Aside from his brilliant DVD documentary, *The Mothman's Photographer*, Colvin has published *nine* books related to the phenomenon. He is without doubt the most informed and prolific regarding all things Mothman.

In fact, if even ten-percent of what he claims is "real," the Point Pleasant chaos needs to be rethought.

To illuminate this, I consider Colvin to be as important as John Keel, Jim Keith, and Carl Jung. Colvin combines anthropology, history, religion, conspiracy theory, and even esoterica including Masonic symbolism, the occult, and how these varied disciplines connect. How refreshing to have such insight. Some of the connections he makes, often through synchronous events, are both enlightening and disturbing.

Colvin ties together (for good or ill) military intelligence, industrial concerns such as I.G. Farben, Union Carbide, General Motors, and others, as well as such near-to-Point Pleasant operations as Defense Logistics Agency (mentioned without name by John Keel in *The Mothman Prophecies*) and even the possible origin of "Indrid Cold," who might have been practicing industrial espionage in the Ohio Valley under cover as a "UFO entity."

True, this a lot to swallow. But it delves into actual human endeavor that might very well go a long way in "explaining" what happened in Point Pleasant.

Post-war industry conceivably involved with the creation of cold-fusion, new metals technology, all under the guise of the UFO/Paranormal/MIB mythology.

Upon first discovering these theories (let's face it, they remain so), I experienced a distinct chill. I urge you to reread Keel's *Mothman Prophecies*, *Operation Trojan Horse*, and *The Eighth Tower* (material cut from the original huge *Mothman Prophecies* manuscript was used—with much editing and additions—in *The Eighth Tower*).

I cannot claim Keel was "threatened" (beyond what actually happened in his life), because the aforementioned books were published before *The Mothman Prophecies*. My only claim is that I have read these, and they go into technical detail left out of *Mothman Prophecies*. Why? My feeling is that Keel's publisher wanted *MMP* to be mostly a commercial book, along the lines of *Chariots of the Gods* and similar fare of late sixties and early seventies pop culture—something unsophisticated readers could absorb without being disturbed (a goal certainly not met with *MMP*!).

None of this did Keel any good.

Returning to Colvin, his work raises provocative questions regarding the so-called Men in Black active in West Virginia, Ohio, and elsewhere. My guess is that MIB appeared both menacing and absurd in order to discredit UFO witnesses. This, of course, is the "accepted" theory.

Not a useless one, either. Intelligence agencies, banking on everything from gangster movies ("Yeah ...see, now...say a word and we'll kill ya.") to Cold War paranoia (your neighbor might be a damned Commie!), the heavily industrial, profitable Ohio Valley was fertile indeed for exploitation. After all, who in officialdom would believe anything said by a bunch of hicks?

Where better to test unconventional aerial vehicles, and spread fear in the guise of "government-looking" agents? As first chronicled by Keel, strange people clearly were gathering information—and worse—from locals.

Ohio Valley residents were extremely reluctant to report being questioned by dark-suited strangers who seemed to have intimate knowledge of their lives and foibles. In fact, older locals claim the MIB disturbed them even more than the frequent UFO/paranormal intrusions.

Any way one views these incidents, the innocent victims were hard-working people naturally unprepared for such harassment. Try and imagine, in our new world of absolute surveillance, this happening in your neighborhood.

It can't be easy, or even possible. Popular culture has absorbed and commercialized the MIB. Yet they are reported still, and apparently haven't made any but the most cosmetic changes to their modus operandi.

Personally, though I despise the cliche, it nevertheless holds: "If it ain't broke, don't fix it." Apparently those in covert power know this.

As I write, I'm wearing a T-shirt purchased at the 2009 Mothman Festival (where I met Colvin), upon which is emblazoned the caricature of a Man in Black, warning: "Watch Your Back, For The Men In Black."

Even without them, ours is a world of apparent self-approved data-sharing. Our unasked-for challenge is to learn how to live with this, under the ever-vigilant eyes of national (global) "security."

I admit that the subjects I write about do occasionally bother me (judging by anonymous emails and two outright cyber-attacks, they apparently *really* bother several others with more leisure time than I). How could they not? While I hesitate to name the individual whose book bore the sentence (paraphrasing here): "If you're beginning to publish articles about UFOs, you have just to some readers become 'one of them.'"

I don't like that. I never will—but it's true.

Latent paranoia, especially today in our surveillance/litigation-crazed world, has become "normal." I wish that wasn't a fact (not at all limited to UFO/Paranormal studies!).

The world shouldn't work this way...but it does.

Well before the 1960s events in Point Pleasant, West Virginia, a handful of people were paying attention to anomalous events. Whether they knew of Charles Fort's work doesn't matter. They had superb attention-span.

No one harassed these people, at least not until WWII, when military intelligence—worldwide—had a definite interest. Were UFOs weapons? Hoaxes? From somewhere else? They didn't know, so began a hard-to-define "program" of questioning pilots and any personnel who reported strange events, of which there was no lack.

My uncle, Joseph Grabowski, was a tail-gunner in the B-17 bomber (also known as the Flying Fortress) during WWII. Trust me, if you were in either the nose or tail of the B-17, your ass might be grass. The Germans in their Me-109 fighters knew where to aim, and held back for no man. It didn't help that the nose-cone and tail of the B-17 were enclosed in the then-new Plexiglas (yes, one "s" in the term). Imagine being a teenager, manning a machine gun capable of blasting through concrete, yet transparent to your enemy. While it's true that the B-17 could withstand being nearly perforated by heavy rounds and still come home, the terrible reality is that those in front or back often returned in bloody shreds.

I owe it to Uncle Joe for introducing me to the UFO phenomenon. While he never directly spoke so, he gave me a hardcover book I still possess: *Inside the Space Ships*, by one George Adamski. I recall being afraid of even opening the book (I was 10 years old), yet managed to closely examine the black-and-white photos of massive, cigar-shaped UFOs. Frankly, I didn't know what to think. Was my gentle uncle trying to tell me something, or simply passing along a book he enjoyed? I don't know. I wish I had access to letters he wrote home to Cleveland during the war. Why? Because Joe—like his brother, my father Stanley—was a stoic, practical sort. No patience for anything related to UFOs, ghosts, etc.

My intuition is that he might have seen the so-called Foo-Fighters—orb-like balls of light that shadowed WWII aircraft (including the Germans, Italians, etc.). We now know that these UFOs did not favor any particular country. American intelligence feared they were some unknown German weapon, unleashed to confuse (since no record exists of Foo-Fighters taking hostile action) enemy aircraft. Certainly, whatever they were, they succeeded, but not to the point of actually sabotaging bomb-runs or aerial surveillance. Based on existing documentation, airmen of all stripes viewed the orbs as mischievous observers.

Photos of Foo-Fighters exist. Google this and you will see.

Aside from the great rock-'n'-roll band of the same name, we'll probably never know what they were.

To my knowledge, and of course I cannot know with certainty, the so-called Foo-Fighters represent original UFO reports coming from military forces. Earlier accounts exist, among the strangest of which might be that from 1928 (from memory...I cannot locate the source, but think it originates with Jacques Vallee outside his *Passport to Magonia*), of an American driving his truck through a rural area and seeing a hexagonal craft, about 30 feet in diameter, with a window behind which stood a normal-looking man gazing down at the witness.

What do these accounts tell us?

1. It is possible, just barely, that German, Italian, Russian, and perhaps American technology had developed a type of null-gravity craft, and were using it for surveillance and/or psychological purposes.

2. I must doubt this, due to the extreme risk of testing prototypes over any populated region. Though 1939 was very close in most people's memory to Orson Welles' "War of the Worlds" radio broadcast, the notion of using this to cover any crash sounds unlikely. It would cause panic.

3. This doesn't rule out such a scenario, but if even one witness existed, that would be enough to spread the word.

4. Are these incidents a case of either/or? Meaning the UFO must have been "one of ours" or "one of theirs"?

5. Given the so-called Trickster Theory so intelligently noted by John Keel, Aimé Michel [17], Jacques Vallee and, more recently, George Hansen [18], might this not represent an authentic unknown, something no one then wanted to deal with? They had no model even for "flying saucers."

6. For what it's worth, these early accounts charge me with a sense of witnesses' authentic encounters with anomalous aerial vehicles.

7. Despite claimed official (however hard to find and ambiguous) denial of such technology, I feel forced to say that they did not have anything in the air so advanced. Obviously I could be wrong.

8. Much has been claimed about at least American technology

that what the public sees is 15 years behind actual state-of-the art.

9. If this is so, why has said-technology not (to public knowledge) been used against very visible, media-covered enemies? Unless we're talking about some ultra-covert devices, nearly impossible to hide, this cannot be a factor. Even those we like to consider "primitive" have cell phones. Thank God, as these have given us perhaps the only window open on various reprehensible atrocities.

While I cannot claim useful knowledge of military advances, I can pass along the following that I feel everyone should know, via James Bamford's book *The Shadow Factory: the Ultra-Secret NSA from 9/11 to the Eavesdropping on America* (2008): "More than three decades ago, when the NSA posed a fraction of the privacy threat it poses today with the Internet, digital communications, and mass storage, Senator Frank Church, the first chairman of the Senate Intelligence Committee, investigated the [National Security Agency] and issued a stark warning: 'That capability at any time could be turned around on the American people and no American would have any privacy left, such [is] the capability to monitor everything: telephone conversations, telegrams, it doesn't matter. There would be no place to hide. If this government ever became a tyranny, if a dictator ever took charge in this country, the technological capacity that the intelligence community has given the government could enable it to impose total tyranny, and there would be no way to fight back, because the most careful effort to combine together in resistance to the government, no matter how privately it was done, is within the reach of the government to know. Such is the capability of this technology.'

"There is now the capacity to make tyranny total in America. Only law ensures that we never fall into that abyss—the abyss from which there is no return."

Reading Bamford's claim that NSA water-cooled supercomputers (as of 2018) will have the capacity to process at exaflop speed (one quintillion—1,000,000,000,000,000,000—operations a second), using power sufficient to run half of a small city, we must admit such information goes well beyond "mind-blowing."

Inserting my neck yet further into the noose, I note that the National Security Agency (aka No Such Agency) began in 1952, an auspicious year for UFO sightings. Make of this what you will, but the agency, charged with Signal Intelligence and other matters, had to have been a nest for reception and analyses of UFO reports. This does not mean NSA worked against the public. Hardly, because someone at official level must pay attention in case national security might be threatened—a simple, pragmatic fact. Here is where I differ from many paying close attention to American intelligence. I have scant awareness of how other countries handle such matters, though American organizations seem "tighter" on this. If UFO phenomena exist (a fair certainty, even to U.S. concerns), then someone must take note. This is how it must be, regardless of all conspiracy-talk. It is in the best interest of any nation to investigate things they don't comprehend. Period.

Yes, I have "issues" with many operations of my country. This doesn't mean I blithely distrust Those In Charge. After all, even the most (theoretically) evil employee must live, might even have a family. This is something, basic as it is, many conspiracy-minded people overlook. Despite what you've seen on *The X-Files*, covert operatives must eat, sleep, and deal with the same stress as "us."

Sharper minds than mine have noted this, particularly John Keel (once accused by the late William Cooper, author of *Behold A Pale Horse*, as being under the thumb of CIA) who understood the machinations of government as befuddled and overwhelmed as any corporation.

Which brings us back to Mothman. Though I cannot possibly defend any MK-ULTRA, mind-control agenda (assuming it was used in West Virginia), I will say that something attached to very human (or inhuman) hands had to have occurred there.

Why? If you take in the countless UFO reports, so many and with such repeatability some residents stopped reporting them, a definite pattern emerges. This is highly unusual. I have in mind the Hudson Valley, New York "black triangle" flap in the 1980s [19]. Anomalous phenomena are almost *never* predictable. Point Pleasant and—on a lesser scale—the Hudson Valley, in this regard stand out.

I recall sitting in the living room with my parents sometime in the late 1980s, watching on TV very strange images of enormous "craft" bearing lights in triangular configuration, defying conventional aircraft explanation. My father said something like:

"This might be bullshit, but whoever's doing it is really good."

At the time I was feeling arrogant, and more than a little impatient with his take. "Dad," I said, "look closer. How can something so large hover silently?" (Of course, I hadn't considered blimps, or similar massive airship prototypes!)

To his credit, my father said. "You're very naive. You want to believe in aliens. You could be wrong."

Actually he said more, most of which is unprintable here. But he was right. Here was the first time I ever saw what looked to me like undeniable proof of the unknown. Way beyond any blurry black-and-white photo in my UFO books. Frankly, the footage scared me. It seemed too real and aggressive. "Wow," I told myself, "this is what you've always wanted to see!" But even though I was an adult, I had to admit I was afraid. This was before I'd heard of Whitley Strieber, whose purported encounters with high-strangeness occurred in the same upstate New York region.

Dad and those days are, sadly, long gone.

But it was unusual for him even to comment. I'm glad he did.

My "take" on all things anomalous in Point Pleasant during the mid sixties, is that they began with genuine paranormal events, and someone with deep pockets was watching. Given that the super-secret NSA was present in southern West Virginia at the Green Banks facility, coincidence is difficult to swallow. As primitive—compared to present-day technology—as the outpost must have been, it was far in advance of anything in use at the time. A "big ear." Green Banks was privy to much communication, meaning, in those days, personal telephone conversations, early facsimile-sends, and of course the entire spectrum of military and TV transmissions.

This does not mean that NSA "caused" any of the Point Pleasant events, but surely must have been aware of them.

It might ring strange, or worse, to admit that I have a lingering fascination. To be cliche, *who* knew *what,* and when did they know it? Were the events exploited? In my informed opinion, almost certainly. Another harsh truth is that sometimes innocent lives are tossed away in the interests of so-called national security (a term rarely, if ever, used in the 1960s). This does not forgive the undoubted subterfuge used against people who probably would not have believed such was active even as it happened. As I learned during my Point Pleasant visits, most locals old enough to remember the events recalled being very afraid of so-called Men in Black, who often showed up at late hours, bearing suspicious and ludicrous credentials. The residents, of course, being hard-working and trusting, took this in with no lack of confusion and concern. Why would they behave otherwise?

I'm thankful nothing on this amazing scale occurred where I was raised. Yes, northeast Ohio had its share of UFO activity and entity reports, but nothing like what happened in the mid to southern part of the state.

I suppose, however unsatisfactorily, it all boils down to this: Something of immense importance happened in Point Pleasant and surrounding areas. Keel documented most of it. But something else was going on, something that hurt many people.

Thanks to investigators such as Andy Colvin, Jim Keith, and several others, we have more insights...but the potent mystery remains.

Cold truth: since most of the original players have passed on, and until someone produces official documents (good luck with that!), we'll never know what actually happened in Point Pleasant, West Virginia.

NOTES:

1. KEEL, John A. *The Mothman Prophecies* (New York; *Saturday Review Press*, 1975; 2002 Tor Edition).

2. http://mothmanlives.com/images/west_virginia_ordnance_works_npl_boundary.jpg

3. *Dark Wings: The Mothman Chronicle*; Black River Films, 2009; DVD documentary.

4. REDFERN, Nick and ROBERTS, Andy. *Strange Secrets: Real Government Files on the Unknown* (Paraview Pocket Books, 2003).

5. KEITH, Jim. *Casebook on the Men in Black* (IllumiNet Press, 1997; Adventures Unlimited Press edition, 2011).

6. BARKER, Gray. *They Knew Too Much About Flying Saucers* (University Books, New York, 1956; New Saucerian Books edition, 2014).

7. MOSELEY, James W. and PFLOCK, Karl. *Shockingly Close to the Truth: Memoirs of a Grave-Robbing Ufologist* (Prometheus Books, 2002).

8. COLEMAN, Loren. *Mothman and Other Curious Encounters* (Paraview Press, 2002).

9. ADAMSKI, George. *Inside the Space Ships* (New York: Abelard-Schuman, 1955).

10. See Chapter 15: The Pentacle Memorandum and Project Stork—(UFO) Game Over?

11. HYNEK, J. Allen. *The UFO Experience: A Scientific Inquiry* (Henry Regnery Company, 1972; Marlowe & Company edition, 1998).

12. COLVIN, Andrew. *The Mothman's Photographer*: *An Andy Colvin Film* (Copyright © 2004 Andy Colvin/Colvin & Chang). A 2-DVD, 12-hour documentary, featuring a 45-minute interview with John A. Keel during the 2003 Mothman Festival in Point Pleasant, West Virginia.

13. www.mothmanmuseum.com/

14. www.markpellington.com/

15. *The Mothman Prophecies* (Lakeshore Entertainment; 2002).

16. WAMSLEY, Jeff. *Mothman: Behind the Red Eyes* (Mothman Press, 2005).

17. MICHEL, Aimé. *Flying Saucers and the Straight-Line Mystery* (S.G. Phillips, 1958).

18. HANSEN, George. *The Trickster and the Paranormal* (Xlibris Corporation, 2001).

19. A solid (if slightly slanted toward the Extraterrestrial Hypothesis) chronicle of the Hudson Valley black-triangle sightings can be found in *Night Siege: The Hudson Valley UFO Sightings*, by Dr. J. Allen Hynek, Philip J. Imbrogno, and Bob Pratt (Llewellyn Publications expanded edition, 1998).

4. INVASION OF THE SAUCERMEN

UFOs exist.

No matter who you are, where you live, or what you do, it's likely you know someone who has "seen something."

First, let's define my usage of the acronym: UFO. This stands for Unidentified Flying Object—nothing more. Never has; never will. Thanks to media ignorance of anything requiring more than two or three seconds' consideration, "UFO" has—since long ago—become synonymous with Extraterrestrial Space Vehicle. Not in *this* book; not in any of my articles or blogs. Not even in my novels, novellas, and short stories.

Other writers have tried solving this ET-biased problem by instead using the acronyms UAP (Unidentified Aerial Phenomena), UAV (Unidentified Aerial Vehicle—adding more confusion, as UAV is generally understood to represent Unmanned Aerial Vehicle, known all too well these days as *drone*), and clumsy variations on Anomalous Aerial Phenomena. It's easy to understand any confusion this semiotic ambiguity might cause in general readers merely curious about UFOs/UAPs/UAVs/AAPs!

In short, people report seeing objects in the air (or, occasionally, on the ground) for which they have no model; no name. We call such things UFOs because they are unidentified, flying (though that isn't necessarily a fact), and apparently solid (not always) objects.

Regarding reports of UFO "occupants," these have practically dropped out of whatever liminal existence they once seemingly had. There are of course the relentless, annoying YouTube clips whose barely literate captions claim *Real Alien being coght on film! Most teriffying fotage ever!* Too bad the Internet didn't exist in 1954 at the height of the so-called October UFO wave in France and Italy. We might have been treated to some genuinely shocking imagery, such as that cited in the following accounts from Jacques Vallee's [1] extraordinary *Passport to Magonia: On UFOs, Folklore, and Parallel Worlds* (1969; 1993).

20 October 1954: Parravicino d'Erba (Italy)
Renzo Pugina, 37, had just put his car in the garage when he saw a strange being covered with a "scaly" luminous suit, about 1.3m tall, standing near a tree. The creature aimed the beam from a sort of flashlight at him, and he felt paralyzed, until a motion he made when clenching his fist on the keys seemed to free him. He attacked the intruder, who rose and fled with a soft whirring sound. An oily spot was found at the site.

23 October 1954: Saint-Hilaire-des-Loges (France)
Mrs. Boeuf was coming out of her farmhouse when she saw a luminous disk in the sky and called her family. When everyone saw the object come closer, they locked all doors and spent a sleepless night. They did not observe the object's departure.

24 October 1954: Les Egots (France)
Near Sainte Catherine, a child saw a man emerge from a strange craft. He was "dressed in red, his clothes looked like iron. He walked with his legs stiff, had long hair and a hairy face. His eyes were large, like those of the cows."

26 October 1954: La Madiere (France)
Aime Boussard, 47, a farmer, was suddenly confronted with an

individual of normal height (1.60m) wearing a sort of diving suit with a pale-green light on either side of the helmet. The individual aimed at the witness the beam of two blue lights, and he was thrown backward. No craft was observed.

To present-day readers, such accounts sound at once absurd, frightening, and even silly. Consider, though, that these reports came from rural areas whose residents were unfamiliar with the UFO phenomenon and, in 1954, were very unlikely to have been influenced by movies and/or television. So then, what *did* influence them?

Excepting the ever-present (yet highly improbable) possibility that genuine extraterrestrials piloting nuts-and-bolts craft have been visiting Earth, witness accounts point toward another direction entirely: inner space.

The "ufonauts" appear in accordance with witness's cultural-religious-ethnic matrix. No matter how seemingly impossible, this aspect is present in every entity report on record. As noted by Vallee, UFO occupants (and strange entities seen with no craft reported) behave in America like science-fictional monsters, while European accounts give us beings mischievous and surreal. South American reports often are violent and terrifying. Needless to say, UFOs and their anomalous ilk care nothing for trivial notions of political correctness. The phenomenon does appear to assume aspects already present in the given region's collective unconscious, which leads us well away from the Extraterrestrial Hypothesis and "outer space" beliefs.

This is, of course, anathema—if not blasphemy—to True

Believers in the ETH. Nonetheless, the data stand.

I'm not the first to note that the UFOs-from-outer-space theory simply isn't weird enough to explain the range of encounters.

Investigators, researchers, and writers (myself included) need to use language with precision and clarity. Any prominent study of linguistics and semiotics, such as *Saussure's Third Course of Lectures in General Linguistics*, and Korzybski's *Science and Sanity*, will inform us that language is hardwired into human perception. Simply, what we call a thing makes up its reality. My kitchen table is a "table" because my (American) culture names it so. One might as easily refer to a table as a "four-legged platform." Hence, a "table" remains a table because that is what we call it—we don't look for other explanations and/or definitions for what actually is a "four- (or more) legged platform."

Relevant to UFOs and the spectrum of so-called paranormality, most—though not all—studies (and predictably reckless media treatment) are so heavily laden with biased language such as *alien, extraterrestrial, Grays,* etc., they unwittingly disprove their own theories. Their appears a genuine incapability—or unwillingness—to intelligently explore the field. Mesmerized by sophisticated visuals and effects, casual viewers believe what they see.

More and more, we are becoming shallow, uninformed, anti-intellectual couch-surfers too lazy and distracted by celebrity bullshit and frivolous Internet fare to think for ourselves. As my sorely missed mentor J.N. Williamson used to say, an ignorant populace is ripe for exploitation.

I will, however, qualify that statement by noting that I don't accept any current conspiratorial notions claiming TV networks plan their aggressive tedium in pursuit of some unofficial "mind control" agenda. No. The old "bread and circus" routine has been among us since the Romans invented it: keep the People numb and pacified with spectacle and drama, and they won't notice the actual state of affairs.

The examples I included from the incredible 1954 European UFO wave are typical of most reported, with craft variously described as saucers, cigars, spheres, blobs of light, and occasionally zooming away on luminous blue trails. Many "occupant" reports from this wave are replete with helmeted entities often carrying objects tipped with fierce blue, green, or red lights, or with lights mounted on the head-gear or chest. There is a mix of faceless entities, and "monsters" glaring at witnesses with glowing eyes.

Early investigator/writers, such as Aimé Michel [2], Henri René Guieu [3], and a few others, were the first to notice patterns in the sightings, and to give as much care and attention to witnesses as to the physical aspects of the encounters. The wave is more accurately called the French 1954 Wave (sounds like an avant-garde film festival, eh?), because the majority of reports came from that country. The peak seems to have hit on the 14th of October, and Vallee lists 11 sightings for that day in *Passport to Magonia*. Whatever causes the infinite variety of manifestations was never busier than during that incredible month.

So-called occupant, or entity, reports peaked in the 1950s and

1960s, then dwindled throughout the 1970s—though the American wave in 1973 brought with it a scatter of accounts featuring tall, silver-suited humanoid forms, and shorter, bulbous-headed precursors to what would become in the 1980s "Grays," the generic extraterrestrial biological entity so potently present in papers and books by John Mack [4], David Jacobs [5], Budd Hopkins [6], Whitley Strieber [7] and others following their lead.

How do we account for today's relative paucity of entity reports?

I think the ever-quickening abandonment of organized religion plays a role, as humanity moves deeper into separating itself from wild nature and its enchanting green spaces, into a soulless fragmented existence of media-generated illusions and organized dullness. Simply put, we no longer believe in even the possibility of "redemption" (even if negative) at the whims of otherworldly beings. Our fears come now from technologically spawned threats such as plagues, increasingly intrusive surveillance, and (to believe our governments) ever-present threats of terrorist attack.

Perhaps in some higher dimension, the strangely poetic denizens look down on us and wonder why we've abandoned them.

NOTES:

1. VALLEE, Jacques. *Passport to Magonia: On UFOs, Folklore, and Parallel Worlds* (Contemporary Books, 1969; 1993).

2. MICHEL, Aimé. *Flying Saucers and the Straight-Line Mystery* (S.G. Phillips, 1958).

3. GUIEU, Henri René. *Black-Out On the Flying Saucers* (Preface by Jean Cocteau; Black River, 1956).

4. MACK, John E. *Abductions: Human Encounters With Aliens* (Charles Scribner's Sons, 1994).

5. JACOBS, David M. *The Threat* (Fireside, 1998).

6. HOPKINS, Budd. *Intruders: The Incredible Visitations at Copley Woods* (Ballantine Books, 1987).

7. STRIEBER, Whitley. *Communion* (Avon Books, 1987).

5. ROSWELL R.I.P.

I have probably read as much about the so-called Roswell Incident as anyone. It's hard to ignore, not only because of what it might mean, but why America (indeed, the world) is so obsessed with the matter.

Here's the thing: something crashed near Roswell. What that thing was, no one can (or will) say. In fact, about all one *can* say is that there *was* a coming-to-ground of *something.* True, it's easy to ask: what possibly can one add to the extant literature? This is not a yes-or-no topic, i.e. did something literally fall? It did. What came after is fraught with misinformation, disinformation, mythology, wish-fulfillment, insanity, and guys-who-know-guys-who-knew-a-guy....

I am honor-bound to admit that I respect the very considerable research (no names—you know them all) carried out, often without much or any compensation, by individuals tougher far than your author. Sometimes I think Roswell has become, if not exceeded, the penultimate mystery, akin to that offered by Baigent, Leigh, and Lincoln in their aggravating, evocative, and fascinating *Holy Blood, Holy Grail* [1], wherein the authors make their case for our knowledge of Jesus Christ being incomplete—if not deliberately obscured.

I was raised to respect and "believe in" Catholicism which, in my huffing, grudging way, I've come to agree to disagree with (pardon the grammar). One cannot hope (as in nearly all matters ufological and paranormal) ever to "win" an argument based on emotional belief.

What's that mean? It means I think Christ actually was a flesh-and-blood being, thus no stranger to pain and the simple realities of life. Was he divine? With all due respect to my long-ago catechism teacher/enforcer Sister Bonaventa—*not* her real name—(who smacked my hand with a ruler because she thought I broke a clock), I can't claim an answer. Frankly, I've learned more from independent study than anything she taught. It wouldn't surprise me, were she still among us lucky few, if she ran down the authors of *Holy Blood, Holy Grail* and phoned their parents afterward. No good deed goes unpunished—especially that of *asking questions.*

You see, that's how it is with believers. Tuck in your white shirt, leave questions at the door with your chewing gum. Speaking only from experience, what I learned from catechism is this: *question us and suffer.*

I digress.

So it goes with Roswell. Investigators smarter far than me have done so. I question their motives—hahaha. But I am not above wanting to know *what happened.* Who is? While I can't for the life of me recall who said the following, I'll paraphrase: If an extraterrestrial vehicle came to ground on American soil in 1947, this would not have been kept secret. There simply was no mechanism for the "black-ops" we see now in every exploitative movie and TV show. Yes, the Manhattan Project was successfully hidden. This is because atomic testing—science—is controllable. UFOs and the paranormal are not, which is why so many moronic claims of crashed UFO secrets must be treated as what they are. A technology supposed to be millions (if not billions) of years ahead of us, yet unable to prevent its products—according to the UFO literature—from crashing all over the world!

The phenomena themselves do whatever they want, wherever they want. Only *data* are controllable.

Had some object, undeniably "other," been recovered the USG would have shouted for assistance from whoever they could find. No effort or expense would have been made to hide such an event. The very fact that something about Roswell is, up to present-day, *still concealed*, stands out.

Whatever crashed there is something no one—no one—wants to talk about....

Why? Investigator Martin Cannon [2] (wherever you are) wrote that the device might have been a drone prototype, tasked to deliver chemical/biological/atomic hell on anti-American countries. Or, had it been Russian, Chinese, etc., this definitely would have been immediately classified since the USG could not admit to penetration of American airspace.

New Mexico was well-suited for testing of any mini-apocalypse. V-2 rockets were routinely test-fired there. Cannon goes on to say that if what crashed was some balloon-supported deliverer of toxins, this might explain many mysterious deaths in the region. If indeed this happened, lawsuits might exist to present-day. This would also shed light on some hard-to-trace tales of locals being menaced at gunpoint to turn over crash-site debris. It is well known that government tests involving airborne toxins over populated areas (San Francisco, the Pennsylvania Turnpike) were conducted with no thought to consequences.

I'm not the first to ask: what could be so scary that, in order to forever cover it up, would be officially termed a "flying disk"? If any other writer has made this claim, I'm not aware of it—but would like to be, if anyone has done so. Roswell's solution, I'm certain, is very simple. The cover-up was brilliant. *Let's call the retrieved crash debris a* flying disk. *No one ever will discover the truth—never. Because people looking for "alien" artifacts and bodies will never look any* deeper.

This is why I view Annie Jacobsen's [3] *Area 51: An Uncensored History of America's Top Secret Military Base* with both fascination and suspicion. Like others, I first heard on National Public Radio about the highly regarded journalist and her hefty volume. Jacobsen's brief synopsis on the Roswell mystery covered in her book was incredibly provocative, and certainly responsible for its popularity.

In short, the book chronicles events and activities of which most military aviation history and Area-51 buffs are already aware, with the exception of a satisfying amount of first-hand insider narratives. The vast landscape was—and is—host to development and test-flights of classified aircraft. This is where (to name only a few!) the U-2 spy plane, SR-71 Blackbird, and F-117 Nighthawk (stealth bomber) were born. The Area-51 mythology claims that recovered UFOs are "reverse-engineered" in order to create exotic prototypes. As covered by Jacques Vallee and others, evidence exists that disinfo agents are charged with promoting UFO mythology in order to obscure from the public (and spies both foreign and domestic) unavoidable overflights of unconventional aircraft. Indeed, anyone reading this is aware of reports of triangular, cylindrical, and even old-school saucer-type craft over the Nevada Test Range. I will not belabor this by rehashing, since anyone currently drawing breath more than likely has at least a bare-bones awareness of Area 51 lore.

It is not my place, or desire, to say this is wrong.

This doesn't mean I agree with the methodology of those holding secret keys. After all, their operations have driven a few investigators (like Paul Bennewitz [4]) insane, others arguably to suicide [5], and in a few cases (conceivably Jim Keith; his ex-girlfriend; his publisher at IllumiNet, Ron Bonds; and Danny Casolaro [6]) might even have ended in terminal action—murder.

We live in an explosive world, where those tasked with our defense must keep secret certain aspects of their operations. Those sneaking around Area-51 and similar "secret" bases are only reinforcing the "reverse-engineered" UFO technology tales. If the United States military actually possesses "alien" craft, why are these not used against so-called primitive enemies? Let's face it, these primitives have cell phones and other gear. They photograph every day our twitchy (and deadly) drones. Wouldn't they be the first to inform the world of our evil deception?

That this is not happening says more than rumors about Area-51 and other "secret" bases ever will.

Annie Jacobsen claims to have nailed the "truth" about the Roswell Incident.

This alone demonstrates how easily even serious investigators are baited and hooked. Jacobsen interviewed several very old-school Area-51 alumni who told her that what crashed near Roswell was indeed a disk-shaped deal, and bore occupants with over-sized craniums and huge black eyes—akin to the "Grays" of modern lore. These turned out to be genetically-mutilated teens crafted by Dr. Josef Mengele, the so-called Nazi madman of Auschwitz, in order to terrify American powers.

The author was told by her aged sources that the Russians had anti-gravity technology, and installed the "kids" inside the craft (which supposedly was remotely-piloted over Alaska and into the Lower 48, though this aspect is light on details). Jacobsen's sources claimed to have seen Cyrillic letters etched into some parts of the saucer's interior.

Here is where I—admittedly disappointed—gave up.

Why include obvious Russian symbology in a device designed to "mimic" extraterrestrial technology? This makes no sense whatsoever. True, American Intelligence would *not* have wanted to admit Russian penetration of U.S. airspace. If anything was likely to cause panic, that would have been it. You can't have it both ways: the craft was Russian or the craft was from Out There....

Jacobsen's digging into the Roswell mystery wasn't without value, as she might have learned the location of official documents pertaining to the crash recovery. Why has no one else been able to find these? Jacobsen says they've been searching the wrong places.

"The information has been protected from declassification by draconian Atomic Energy Commission classification rules, hidden inside secret Restricted Data files that were originally created for the Atomic Energy Commission by EG&G [Edgerton, Germeshausen, and Grier]."

Obviously someone isn't talking; or, those who *are* cannot be taken seriously. Whoever *does* know what took place near Roswell aggressively hides the facts. The truth, whatever that might be, is probably shocking, and more full of guilt and shame than anyone ever will admit.

NOTES:

1. BAIGENT, Michael; LEIGH, Richard; LINCOLN, Henry. *Holy Blood, Holy Grail* (Delacorte Press, 1982; Delta edition, 2004).

2. CANNON, Martin. "Roswell: Truth and Consequences" (Article, 1996) http://www.redshift.com/~damason/lhreport/articles/roswell.html

3. JACOBSEN, Annie. *Area 51: An Uncensored History of America's Top Secret Military Base* (Back Bay Books, 2012).

4. BISHOP, Greg. *Project Beta: The Story of Paul Bennewitz, National Security, and the Creation of a Modern UFO Myth* (Gallery Books, 2005).

5. GENZLINGER, Anna and COLVIN, Andrew B., Editor. *The Jessup Dimension* (New Saucerian Books, 2014).

6. THOMAS, Kenn and KEITH, Jim. *The Octopus: Secret Government and the Death of Danny Casolaro* (Feral house; revised edition, 2003).

6. THE REAL KEEL DEAL

The late John A. Keel had as many detractors as supporters. Even his critics must admit that Keel, often at his own expense, traveled most of America in order to meet with and interview witnesses to the unknown.

Keel did so not out of some personal belief-system, but out of natural curiosity and more than a little concern. He had, as a youngster hanging out in his parents' barn in Perry, New York, a brief yet powerful experience about which most of his readers know nothing.

Keel's home was rural and isolated, so prevented him from engaging in the usual activities of others. As mentioned in *Jadoo* [1], his 1957 book chronicling journeys in Egypt, Tibet, India and elsewhere, in search of "magic" and other secrets, the 20-something man craved experience and thrills.

In the old barn, Keel noticed a scratchy thump against the wood. He said aloud: "Knock once for yes, twice for no."

Whatever was present complied, giving the teen his first taste of the unknown. This frightened him, and ignited the spark of his life's long, strange journey.

Keel's parents, though not abusive, did not support his literary interests, and one day he packed a small box and left home at age 17. "So on a hot summer day in 1947 I packed a few things into a cardboard box and walked downstairs, a queasy feeling in my stomach. My mother looked at me, startled. 'Aren't you going out to the hay field today?' she asked.

"No. I'm going away," I said simply....

"It was four years before I saw her again. And then only for a brief two-week period before I went into the Army."

Keel hitched into Pennsylvania and ended up in New York City, barely a dollar in his pocket. So began a hand-to-mouth existence, hanging out with poets, crackpots, and artists of the Beat generation. He became the unpaid editor of a poetry magazine, and "...slowly I gained a toehold on the writing business, churning out such intriguing hack articles as: 'Are You A Repressed Sex Fiend?' and 'Will Sex Become Obsolete?' before I managed to land steady assignments writing continuity for comic books...

"Then the Korean war broke out and I was drafted."

What happened after is the stuff of Keelian history.

Despite being American and white, and over six-feet-tall, the young man managed to talk himself into many fascinating—and dangerous—situations. Keel's search for genuine magic rarely was fulfilled, as he learned that many so-called secrets were shams. He tried, and failed, to reproduce the classic "rope-trick," the claimed extra-human ability for a man to actually climb up a rope. It was possible, of course, if one knew the "trick."

But Keel, in Tibet, did claim to witness both telekinesis and levitation he could not explain. I credit him for sticking with his life-long practicality, something that mostly benefited him later (investigating the Mothman events, for one).

After my first reading of *The Mothman Prophecies*, I found myself disturbed and skeptical. Years later, after reading *Jadoo*, I had a quite different take.

Here was a guy, very intelligent and practical, who actually had the courage to seek answers to questions that fascinated him, and discovered most of these ancient "secrets" were bullshit. It must have hurt to see, excepting a few apparently authentic experiences, the anticipation of magic crushed before a man in his early 20s.

This put a whole different "spin" on *The Mothman Prophecies*. Some positive, some not.

After all, a man who had traveled far, putting his very life on the line, was impressive; and is still. Keel himself, upon hearing of the Point Pleasant events, admitted much doubt. But he took these seriously, armed with knowledge of the potential for hoaxing, and how much easier it might be to "put one over" on Americans unaware of Eastern "secrets."

I am not the first to note that Keel could have exaggerated certain aspects of the UFO, MIB, Mothman activity. Too, he had the skills to convince nearly anyone of anything. But he chose not to pursue that reprehensible path.

As much as I admire aspects of Gray Barker [2] (conceivably responsible, in his 1956 book *They Knew Too Much About Flying Saucers*, for creating the Men-in-Black active mythology), ample evidence exists that he had a hand in some of the telephonic, MIB harassment—perhaps even of Point Pleasant residents during the Mothman/UFO events.

I'll just come out with it: I loathe hoaxers and the unnecessary trouble they cause. Who can say how many lives were either disrupted or ruined in the guise of "a good time"?

The cliche works: You're part of the problem, or part of the solution.

Barker, at least before 1960, attempted both. He pissed off many, Keel included. But Keel at least gave Barker the benefit of the doubt, even after he'd discovered that Barker was responsible for a handful of bizarre telephone nonsense. Barker wrote, and published, some very interesting books. Then again, as noted by James Moseley and Keel, for some mysterious reason he "gave up," and started having fun. While I am certainly not worthy of denying Barker his frolics, I wish he had given more thought to their consequences.

In my estimation, Keel summed up what all others have missed: UFOs/paranormal phenomena are real. They exist and are a normal aspect of our environment. *What they might actually be we do not, probably cannot, know.* Behind these events exists an intelligence both disturbing and powerful—nearly "godlike." There is as much evidence for hostile "intent" as there is for "good."

I am not a believer. But I think Keel had it right. All of these things share a common source, most of which originates in humankind, but with some unknown external trigger—which could be anything from extraterrestrials to interdimensional intelligences to something as yet unimagined. Or even some heretofore unrecognized earth-based phenomenon. Whatever it might be is undoubtedly energetic, occasionally luminous, stealthy, and deceptive. It has no interest in allowing us to know its origin, hence the absurd and ultimately useless statements of "spirits" and "spacemen." One can review transcripts from trance-mediums and the "contactees" from the 1950s and 1960s, up to present-day abductees, and see how these function. Everything the voices say (excepting a few accurate predictions, nothing to be sniffed at) is either a lie or a deception.

The fact that such voices occasionally give genuine data points toward an answer, if not a total solution. They *know* about us because they *come* from us. I find this possibility as confounding and fascinating as any theory regarding sentient beings from this universe.

To label John A. Keel's 1975 *The Mothman Prophecies* a "classic" is like calling a Jaguar XJ "good transportation." Across decades, from music-obsessed teen to full-time writer/editor, I have observed the book's divisive effect on readers. Too, I have noticed another effect: astonishment, mingled with fear.

At 17, many things were working to open my mind, but Keel's utterly entrancing—and terrifying—account of Point Pleasant, West Virginia's besiegement by a William Corliss [3] catalog of anomalies, the winged Mothman as host, detonated in my skull.

To my much-younger self, residing in northeast Ohio (under four hours' drive-time from Point Pleasant), Keel's journalistic deadpan frightened me with its apparently nonfictional descriptions of pure nightmare: Mothman, the 7-foot-tall winged entity with eyes glowing red like bicycle reflectors...sinister MIB whose gushing threats were only amplified by absurd behavior...UFOs studded with prismatic lights, menacing the skies as if scheduled...isolated homes terrorized by the cries of invisible babies in dead gray hours...pounding poltergeists...bizarre telephone calls...and Keel's dawning dread that someone, or some thing, knew in advance his every move, even mimicked him both telephonically and physically.

I'll tell you, more than any other book, *The Mothman Prophecies* profoundly affected how I viewed the world, at once disturbed me and opened my mind to dark forces churning behind the days.

What made the read bleaker still was my recalling—well into it —watching television on 15 December 1967, when network news interrupted to tell us that the Silver Bridge—laden with rush-hour traffic—had collapsed into the icy black waters of the Ohio River.

Decades later, at the 2003 Mothman Festival in Point Pleasant, I briefly met John Keel, on his way out of a shop where he had been signing books—*lots* of books. I didn't then know about his failing vision, attributing his guarded stride to age. How tall he was! I'm 5 feet 11 inches, and Keel had a few on me. His white suit, black shirt, and white tie stood out among the hundreds of attendees, as if Keel were still flipping the bird (pun intended) at his old enemies by presenting as an anti-MIB. Perhaps he was.

I visited Point Pleasant, and surrounding areas, four times more, explored the vast TNT area where once stood the North Power Plant, site of the (in)famous 15 November 1966 Mothman sighting by Linda and Roger Scarberry, and Steve and Mary Mallette. This 3,655-acre range, about seven miles north of Point Pleasant, is also known as the McClintic Wildlife Management Area, and has required over the years much reclamation to restore the ponds and fields and woods from industrial toxins recklessly handled during World War II, when the region was called the West Virginia Ordnance Works and site of explosives production.

Walking and driving in the TNT area (especially at night) is a soul-tweaking experience. Miles and miles of lightless narrow roads, populated with creaking crickets and trees hissing in the wind. It isn't hard to believe practically *anything* might happen, and no one the wiser. Keel described its silent desolation with masterful precision, and during the Mothman/UFO activity spent countless hours alone there. Even local police feared joining him.

Another aspect of *The Mothman Prophecies* that chilled me was Woodrow Derenberger's [4] account of his 2 November 1966 meeting with alleged ufonaut Indrid Cold, on then new Interstate 77 near Parkersburg, WV (not far from where I now live). My family, then living in the Cleveland, Ohio suburb of Solon, traveled that same highway during summer vacations throughout the 1960s.

I am not a "believer," in the sense accepted by Magonians and Forteans alike, but do think something occurred in Point Pleasant, some of which might have involved genuine anomalies. But, like the late Jim Keith and still-on-this-side-of-the-ground Andy Colvin (author of the *Mothman's Photographer* series of books, and producer of a 12-hour documentary), I think the town was selected for an ambitious psyops program, perhaps associated with some MK-ULTRA sub-project or—more likely—Project Stork (conceived in nearby Columbus, Ohio). After all, Defense

Logistics Agency once had a facility there.

It is sad to know how little Keel benefited, financially, from the book's publication. This would eventually be remedied—decades later—when it was optioned for film production.

I have read *TMMP* many times, referred to it for my own writing—fiction and nonfiction, and it holds up quite well. Sure, that scoundrel Gray Barker was responsible for a few hoaxes, and Keel busted him for most of them. Even after watching the PBS Gray Barker documentary, *Shades of Gray*, I find the man's behavior inexplicable, though do value his very early work.

John Keel, at least in my mind, never was burning so bright as during the writing of *TMMP*. Hell, he actually gave us two books, as the publisher considered Keel's original manuscript too thick. Keel published—after additional editing and writing—this "left-over" material as the equally classic (if more sober) *The Eighth Tower*, recently reissued by Anomalist Books.

Above all, John A. Keel taught me a dark truth: "The universe does not exist as we think it exists. We do not exist as we think we exist."

Take that, cynics.

And, rest him well, I owe this philosophy to the considerable, mostly unheralded, efforts of John Alva Keel.

NOTES:

1. KEEL, John A. *Jadoo* (Julian Messner, Inc., 1957; Anomalist Books edition,2013).

2. www.theyknewtoomuch.com/

3. William Corliss (1926-2011) was an American physicist and writer who, among other books, researched and wrote the Sourcebook Project, beginning in 1974 and comprised of a number

of volumes listing unusual phenomena culled from scientific journals.

4. DERENBERGER, Woodrow with HUBBARD, Harold W. *Visitors From Lanulos* (Vantage Press, 1971; Point Pleasant, 2014).

7. THE GOBLIN BARRIER

Confounding and bizarre, the perceived rift between anomalous aerial phenomena (UFOs) and paranormal events (ghosts, poltergeist activity, psychic visions, etc.) remains an unnecessary —even tragic—fact in field investigation.

I use the term *perceived* because there is no "physical" gap between these—only a subjective one, found usually in those ignorant of the vast (admittedly uneven) literature piled up over hundreds of years, a lot of this by organizations whose names might surprise some of you: the Vatican; Russian intelligence (scientific, well-funded, deadly serious); CIA (even a partial listing of MK-ULTRA sub-projects would run many pages); FBI; universities with corporate, private, and government funding. Regardless of any of these having individual ambitions and agendas, they gathered—a few continue to gather—reams of raw data.

Out of that (short) list, probably the Vatican keeps the largest collection, and might very well have been the first to note a continuum between "lights in the sky" and ground-based phenomena, divine or otherwise. Poltergeist activity (rock-throwing, unaccountable movement of inanimate objects, "apports" such as falls of coins, biologicals, etc.) is recorded as far back as AD 400, well before anyone thought of exploiting such matters for personal or political gain.

Some researchers think Vatican scholars were and are coerced to "accept" only those accounts that reinforce the Roman Catholic church, i.e., "Our miracles are better than yours—and approved!" An obvious absurdity, akin to those uttered by government conspiracy-mongers who believe fabulous UFO artifacts and secrets are under lock and key. No one can control, or hide, a global phenomenon so fugitive, culturally adaptive, and incomprehensible.

What *can* be controlled is disclosure of gathered data—nothing more. It might be very interesting if American intelligence released their files, as did the UK not long ago. But *data is not information.* I have read a sampling of Ministry of Defense documents, and they offer a confused, often annoyed, record of meandering nocturnal lights, bright stars, jarring cries in empty buildings, mysterious "animals," and apparently solid but obscure objects seen in daylight. I doubt American documents tell a different story.

Photographs, be they of unusual machines in the sky or on the ground, apparitions, or cryptids (unknown and/or "paraphysical" creatures) can never prove anything. This was true in the twentieth century; even more so now. A photograph tells us nothing useful about its subject. In today's slippery high-tech environment— forget it. There are even apps [1] for iPhones and/or Android for creating fake UFO photos: UFO Camera Gold, UFO Revelator, and UFO Photo Bomb—to name but three.

None of this discounts that we share a world thrumming with anomalies. In our skies, lakes, seas, homes, and minds. I agree with that old, bespectacled, brilliant and often pissed-off Charles Fort, whose four classic tomes—*The Book of the Damned*, *New Lands*, *Lo!*, *Wild Talents*—first collected from newspapers, university and science journals, accounts of all things Damned.

Fort hated believers, scientists, charlatans, and petty authority; the whole "either/or" mindset. He posed the question: Not *if* such things exist—but *why*?

In Fort's world there existed no Goblin Barrier. But a timeless march of weirdness forever just out of reach, a few decades ahead of common wisdom. "A procession of the damned. By the damned, I mean the excluded. We shall have a procession of data that Science has excluded. Battalions of the accursed, captained by pallid data that I have exhumed, will march. You'll read them—or they'll march. Some of them livid and some of them fiery and some of them rotten...."

Fort wrote the above in 1919.

Sometimes, I'm sure nothing since then has changed.

NOTES:

1.http://www.csicop.org/si/show/ufo_hoaxes_theres_an_app_for_that

2. FORT, Charles. *The Book of the Damned* (first published 1919; Jeremy P. Tarcher/Penguin collected edition, 2008).

8. DRONE IN LOVE WITH YOU

You may have noticed the escalation of UFO sightings between 2010 and present day. I certainly have, and had until recently spent several hours each week scanning news-feeds. Finally, enough was enough.

I give no great credence to Internet material, but it does provide literally hundreds of hours, on any given week, of cell phone footage. It's too late to complain, so I merely pay attention, as though personally taking time to stand outdoors with my (nonexistent) BlackBerry. Let's get something out of the way. I hate cell phones, even though I had the chance to be among the first, in 1992, to own one. My then-employer settled for my keeping a "beeper" at my side, in case some black-clad terrorist decided to attack our aggressively bland company.

Personal angst aside, I do understand I ought to be grateful that most of you possess cell phones. I *am* grateful. Why? Because some of you, between texting what you ate for lunch, are capturing anomalous aerial objects. All I can say is "wow." You're getting some stuff people in the 20th century would have killed for, had they the technology.

The real problem rears its head, as it must, when said technology is mishandled. As you know, we have some talented bastards out there, devious and empty-headed. A terrible combination. The same type who have punked UFO investigators, journalists, and even military charges (who mostly hate even having to take UFOs seriously). Google "UFO photos" and you'll find hundreds of thousands, some so good you might reach into the photo and brush your fingers across silvery metal, or even the tight-fitting suits of UFO occupants. Many, however, are obvious trash, expecting the viewer actually to believe the images are authentic.

I've seen these. So have you. But seeing definitely is not—I hope—believing.

As earlier mentioned, a photograph—even of a "genuine" anomaly—proves nothing. Visuals are visuals—nothing more. These can never tell us where the object originated, who's in charge, or what intentionality might have brought the thing our way.

As the Metallica song proclaims: sad but true.

I have seen a *lot* of video footage taken of strange aerial objects; 90% of this must be drones [1], because they're seen hovering over military bases, banks, reservoirs, power plants, schools, and large cities. They cannot be extraterrestrial vehicles, because these would have no need whatsoever even to penetrate our atmosphere. As noted by Jacques Vallee [2], a human-manufactured satellite the size of a beer keg could gather in mere hours enough data to inform its makers of every important activity on Earth, with no landings. Vallee observed this decades ago. Now we have personnel living on orbiting space stations.

I am not aware of even a single report from these platforms

claiming to have seen UFOs entering our atmosphere, though there are accounts of space-borne anomalies. These are genuinely weird, and YouTube offers plenty of streaming video for the curious. NASA's explanations (when they bother to offer them) will deflate the tires of those looking for confirmation of ET activity.

I think NASA keeps many images out of public scrutiny, but not for any conspiratorial reasons. I've reviewed some awfully strange images taken of the lunar surface, from both the light side and the far side (as you ought to know, there is no *dark* side of the Moon). Many, undoubtedly, are nothing more than terrestrial leavings and wreckage; but not all. Some things cannot be hidden, but that doesn't mean their origin is extraterrestrial. Silvery cones, disks, stitch-like tracks exist. Several anomalies resemble domes which, if real, must be hundreds of miles in diameter. As an amateur astronomer since 1978, I have spent considerable time eyeing the lunar surface and its silent beauty, and have spotted a few of these anomalous features (I hesitate to call them objects like some others have). What they might represent, I cannot say, but certainly they are very provocative. Perhaps many of the things in the photos are artifacts and glitches in the imaging process; some probably are fakes. A hell of a lot of them have proved, after thorough analysis, to be reflections and/or shadows enhanced by boulders, crater rims, rills, and other elements of the terrain.

Drones are now a fact, used most prominently against those in league with terrorist agendas. I recall buying a magazine several months after 9/11 featuring photos of "early" drones, one of which obviously was a prototype for the Predator so ubiquitous in present-day media. Military technology, from all accounts, is 15 years ahead of publicly displayed artifacts. Example: the F-117 stealth fighter was on the drawing boards—so to speak—in the early 1970s, and "outed" by a single photograph in the late 80s. This vehicle was often reported, during test-flights in Nevada, as a UFO. Hard to believe, but I have witnessed a daylight flyover of the Stealth, and can easily see it, in darkness, taken as a UFO— regardless of its fairly loud engines. The B-2 bomber, basically a flying wing, was a strange sight, but noisy. Viewed at night, you wouldn't long mistake it for a UFO.

Which brings us to the subject of the so-called black triangle UFO, so prominent during the Hudson Valley, New York UFO flap of roughly 1984 to 1987—but apparently still active.

So much has been written about what these objects might, or might not, be, any chance of objectivity is lost. While I have no intention of replaying the events, I will recount the basics. Hundreds of people in the Hudson Valley, about one hour north of New York City, reported seeing a (usually) gigantic triangular craft with green, red, and white lights at each point. Some claimed to have stood directly under this craft, and saw a red plasma-like light. Most of the reports—save a very few—mention the craft as being silent. This, at the very least, ought to flag the object(s) as a dirigible.

You may have seen on TV the famous video-footage shot by one Hudson Valley resident. Clearly, we can see a dark triangular form dimly illuminated by lights at each point, heading east with little more than a subdued humming. As my late father remarked,

"That humming should tell us something." I know what it tells me. The UFO, no matter its size, very probably was a dirigible—a blimp. What else, of tremendous size, could move so leisurely, even hover? It's often reported, too often, in UFO sightings, that the craft was "as big as a football field." Have you ever stood beneath a blimp? I have. Growing up near Cleveland, Ohio, I often saw the Goodyear blimp (based in Akron, some 30 miles south) as it nosed toward Cleveland to provide news-coverage of sporting events in the stadium there. Once, around 1970, the blimp had engine trouble, and came near to ground at the abandoned airfield half a mile down the road from my home. Every boy in the neighborhood dropped whatever he was doing and ran over to see this rare spectacle—myself among them. My point: based on sound, I would not have known the blimp—200 feet in length— even was there, had one of my pals not telephoned me.

In darkness, no one would have seen it.

I cannot be certain this explains the Hudson Valley sightings, but I'm pretty sure it does. I have a book from 2001 stating that dirigibles might be used to transport troops. And then as now, large airship prototypes exist.

I know that doesn't entirely explain away what was seen in the Hudson Valley, and—to present day—many other places. Too, some "high-strangeness" elements were reported. Triangular UFOs have been reported as long ago as the 1960s. Were these early drones?

As early as the 1960s, many UFO reports might have been solved by inserting "drone" for "UFO." But no model, in the public eye, yet existed for this. Our present world is absolutely alien to that of the 1980s, for good or ill.

In my guise as a writer of short fiction and novels, I often try to imagine how someone from the 1960s—or 1970s—might react were he transported to our time. My guess: total shock. Not at anything as trivial as clothing (though that would stand out), but at the pace of our ordinary lives. The unfortunate traveler would more than likely end up sick by the end of his or her first day in our manic, media-controlled run, where nothing is actually real, even daily news, spun-out and topped by some other disaster within the hour. I can barely handle writing about this.

People are seeing many odd things in the skies these days, similar to the UFO waves of 1952, 1966, 1973, 1984, etc. Existentially, these days are nothing at all like those.

I would estimate that out of every 100 UFO sightings, 95% can be explained by drones employed by military, government, law enforcement, and obscure or even covert institutional and corporate concerns. Let's face it, most of these can afford the hyper-thread, massively parallel-processing computers necessary to drive their water-cooled data farms.

The most radical, hard-edge drones are no larger than a dragonfly. Expensive? Yes. Out of the question?

No.

NOTES:

1. http://dronecenter.bard.edu/publication/the-drone-primer/
2. VALLEE, Jacques. *Dimensions: A Casebook of Alien Contact* (Ballantine Books, 1989; Anomalist Books edition, 2008).
3. http://rationalwiki.org/wiki/Lunar_anomalies

9. WHERE ART MEETS MYSTICISM

What I'm attempting is a sort of deconstruction of so-called paranormal phenomena. No, I am not the first to possess such "ambition." Hardly. I may, however, be one of the last, in a world with no attention-span.

So it goes.

I have noticed that, for some reason, the wisdom of Carl Jung is dismissed by many earning their bread in the same field. I don't know why this is, for I think Jung was among the first outside the field of parapsychology to deliver, through intense research, extremely valuable ideas. Perhaps his arrow came too close to striking the target of what it means to be human. Many of his critics seem to overlook the workman-like precision Jung employed. The difficult, sheer repetitiveness necessary to establish testable results. Yet Jung carried out the heavy-lifting no one else, at the time, was willing to do.

What does this mean? Jung discovered, through thousands of sessions, that there exists an undeniable continuum in the dream-lives of all people—regardless of background, income, or race. He pursued this to his death in 1961. Jung's *Man and His Symbols* [1] was the last work undertaken by a man who wanted general readers to understand *that the imaginative life must be taken seriously in its own right, as the most distinctive characteristic of human beings.* Beyond any doubt, Jung was the first authoritative figure even to consider paranormal phenomena.

His work has since been beaten down, mostly by those promoting "external" (i.e. demonic, apparitional, extraterrestrial) influence as an explanation for anomalous events. I must admit he may have been wrong—but not completely. Jung himself experienced a number of uncanny, even aggressive, "weird" happenings. The most well-known being his meeting with Freud, during which poltergeist-like activity splintered one of Jung's bookshelves. Talk about synchronicity! That incident alone ought to establish that *we* have much to do with "paranormal" frights. Jung himself remained unsure, but knew there must be a connection; that the spectrum of our consciousness was more powerful than previously known.

If only he'd had another decade, he may very well have figured the paranormal. Sadly, his research failed to withstand the "occult" pop-culture of the 1960s. Or did it really fail? I urge you to read Jung. He *didn't* fail, because he set others on the same path.

Here is where Jung's extensive work pays off. Undoubtedly others were pursuing the "unconscious" line as being in charge of the paranormal. One aspect of this always leaves me asking: why? In recordings of so-called spiritual mediums, what stands out are the messages from the "dead." Across the board, these are absurd, even boringly repetitive, yet believed as proof of life after death. If the "ghosts" knew so much, why did they repeat the same ridiculous dialogue (as they do still)?

Could it be these voices came from the human collective

unconscious? This would explain how they know certain facts, yet get unnecessarily confused. Jung knew this was far more interesting than "ghosts," but few wanted to accept that. Given present-day access to the literature of so-called seances, anyone can read transcripts and see that "spirits" often repeated themselves with unvarying predictability. When asked "Is there a God?", the response often was, "Do you want there to be" or "If there were, wouldn't I tell you?" Never an absolute answer. Hard as it may be to accept, this continues today. But TV producers don't want that.

Fact: the voices are real. Fact: they are predictable. This hasn't changed, nor is it likely to.

The entire tradition of exploitation (unchanged for hundreds of years) is too strong, banking on simple human sadness and pain. To the "medium" or "channeler" it's all the same. An easy income. The few authentic "voices" that come through make no sense, and terrify the receivers. You don't need me to recall TV shows wherein "ghost-hunters" claim to have captured voices—popularly known as EVP, for Electronic Voice Phenomena. "I died in the war," etc. I have heard these. So have you. But all the teams I've seen on TV never make recordings under RF- (radio frequency) screened conditions, so could just as easily be capturing digital artifacts of the process, ambient electromagnetic chaff, cross modulation, or are hoaxers.

But what are we to make of technologically "secure" recordings of EVP?

Perhaps the most worthwhile work in EVP was done by Konstantïns Raudive [2] (a student of Jung) and Hans Bender.

They recorded over 100,000 audio-tapes, which they had listeners outside the project confirm as reproducing verifiable, if bizarre and oddly parsed, voices.

Current explanations for EVP, in addition to those cited above, are faulty ground loops, white-noise filtering (the process of which produces a swooshing effect similar to that of a wah pedal used on an electric guitar, and manifests as vowel-like sounds), and auditory pareidolia—"Rorschach audio." The most telling aspect, oft-cited by hardcore skeptics, is the simplest: investigators hear the voices in their (the investigators') own language.

I have experimented—indoors and outdoors—with various devices to capture EVP, and had limited success. Results from the outdoor sessions require much more space than I have here, and consent from others before I can publish them. Indoors, I captured two events (after 20 hours of recording); one resembling a muffled moan like someone weeping; the second I interpreted as "...we are awash..." or "...we are watched..." The swooshing quality bothers me, but the voice does sound recognizably male. Regarding EVP, all I can offer is that my personal jury is still out....

Here is where art meets mysticism. Charlatans back off.

As noted in my Introduction, *people* are the most haunted elements in existence; another aspect Jung (and his students, most prominently Aniela Jaffé) noticed. There will always be a fascination with the unknown, but Jung died convinced most of this comes from *us*. I think he was on the right track which, to my way of thinking, only exults the mysterious profundity of human consciousness. I would like to have the answers. Who wouldn't?

Not until reading *Man and His Symbols* did I feel Jung had nailed the essential question: *Why do paranormal events carry such absurd weight?*

I am honor-bound to say that if your knowledge of "the paranormal" comes from TV and movies and novels, well, you're on the wrong track. The reality—such as it is—has nothing to do with these. Paranormal events are both more disturbing, and mundane, than most will ever know. But we live in a world addicted to sensationalism and vapid drama. No screenwriter (well, most) wants the "facts." Simply, these are often surprisingly trivial.

Though it has taken a long time for me to get here, I couldn't fairly have done so without relating the previous material. Reading Jung, and how he connects abstract art (Pollock, Miro, etc.) to mysticism began as quite a stretch. What I most admire about Jung and his students is that not one claimed to have "the answer," but Jung himself must have known how close they were getting.

For instance, there is in Jung's last book a photograph of a Jackson Pollock [3] painting. You might think you don't know Pollock, but you do. His "action paintings" sparked the spatter-paint-anywhere-and-call-it-art debate over the value of abstract, non-representational paintings. Different from his early work, Pollock's famous paintings are chaotic and anti-structural—protean tangles vibrant with layered color, as though done by a child. The truth is that Pollock was working from his own unconscious, beyond intellect and technique. Jung's book includes a photograph of a metal vibrating plate where sound waves are visible. They precisely resemble a Pollock. How did the artist "know" this?

Answer: he didn't—on the conscious level. This connection exemplifies what has been termed "quantum connectedness." Charles Fort would have had a hoot with this.

Here is where the line between the paranormal and creativity dissolves.

That it exists at all is doubtful; like something imposed by the overly intellectual. I'm not the first to notice resemblances between reported UFO entities, or occupants, and figures portrayed in both abstract and surreal art. On the other hand, maybe I am. Only Jacques Vallee has noted the "poetic" strangeness of some reports. But you will not find such reports coming from America or England. What does that tell us?

I know what it tells me. There must be, for lack of a better term, a connection between human consciousness (meaning dreams, fears, hopes, etc.) and the manifestations of UFO entities and free-ranging "elementals." It took not long for me to recognize in Vallee's *Passport to Magonia* (which lists UFO landing reports from 1868 to 1968) that these things appeared in accordance with the "accepted" culture of the given times. Witnesses described robot-like humanoids, often faceless, who, when they spoke at all, said absurd things: "What is your time?" and "We only want to take you to a different place"; "We are from everywhere" and countless other nonsense.

There are descriptions of beings "wrapped in plastic, with green glowing eyes." Anything one might imagine. Again, I am not the first to notice this, but genuine flesh-and-blood beings from an extra-solar biosphere would not breathe our air and walk on two legs. Given the infinite complexities of evolution, the odds against this are astronomical. Many witnesses described the entities as disoriented, like lost ghosts, and lacking any sense of individuation or integrated personality.

The "faceless" aspect is most reported in the late 1950s through much of the 1960s, after the culture had thoroughly—if only in a visual sense—absorbed abstract painting and other art produced by artists haunted by mysterious figures poised in often bleak landscapes cluttered with emotionally charged objects from daily life. A brief search of "surrealism" on Google will easily conjure many examples of such forms from Dali, Miró [4], De Chirico, and similar others. I noticed this (back in the bawdy 1970s) on record-album art from electronic musicians such as Klaus Schulze [5], Gong, Hawkwind and others.

My point is that these images, unnoticed by most, existed in marginal/underground scenarios. Whether the UFO entities inspired this or vice versa really doesn't matter. A continuum clearly exists. The real question is *why.*

Perhaps these faceless figures represent a collective spiritual despair, a fear of the individual being submerged in the mindless masses. I cannot claim I want this to explain every weird event, every vision of a UFO occupant, because that is not enough.

Which leads us back to Carl Jung, and his idea that *we* create our gods, and ghosts, for good or ill.

NOTES:

1. JUNG, Carl G., Editor; and after his death von FRANZ, M.-L. *Man and His Symbols* (Dell Publishing, 1968).
2. RAUDIVE, Konstantïns. *Breakthrough: An Amazing*

Experiment in Electronic Communication With the Dead
(Taplinger Publishing Company, 1971).
   3. www.jacksonpollock.org/
   4. http://joanmiro.com/
   5. www.klaus-schulze.com/welcome.htm

10. BACK IN THE DAY

Though it might be difficult for readers new to UFO literature to accept, sightings similar to modern-day accounts are present in reports much older.

I realize most UFO studies currently available emphasize phenomena that began in 1947, with the Arnold [1] sighting and Roswell Incident. This is nothing less than an insult to any intelligent person curious about anomalies, and about UFO phenomena in particular, because accounts exist in literature from nearly all countries—some predating the Bible.

Critics and debunkers of UFO reality often point toward old accounts as unreliable and even useless. They are wrong.

Out of all we might consider lacking in ancient peoples, we are wrong to view them as primitive and ignorant. True, they did not benefit from the digital and optical technology of our day, but they were very aware (in a way beyond modern understanding) of night skies and their wonders.

Example: how many people do you know who can even point out simple objects—Mars; the brightest star in Northern skies, Sirius; or even Venus, the "morning star," glaringly brighter than anything but the Moon?

Part of the problem, it is true, is due to light-pollution. Very few so-called dark-sky locations exist in America. However, the objects mentioned are clearly visible even from Times Square in New York City. This doesn't mean anyone bothers to notice.

My point here is that "ancient" peoples were very conscious of the night sky. They did not have streetlights, or indeed any kind of light to blind them. It is true that most retired at dark, in order to wake to begin their toil. Therefore, anything unusual in the sky would stand out. It is sad that few accounts exist of the daily lives of ancient people, but that doesn't really matter. Oddly, there are many reports of poltergeists, ghosts, and natural anomalies such as falls from the skies of rocks, living creatures, strange-colored hail and ice, and bizarre weather. These reports are strikingly similar to those of the present day, long before anyone cared (or dared?) to give them scientific scrutiny.

Which leads to a conclusion (perhaps deduction is more accurate); one, I must admit, I wanted no part of for many years: *Anomalous phenomena are a normal, if unsettling, condition of the planet.*

Charles Fort, in his absolutely groundbreaking *The Book of the Damned* (1919; many reprints), was first to publish this genuinely original notion. When confronted with Fort's universe of data, the aforementioned *Book of the Damned*; *New Lands* (1923); *Lo!* (1931); and *Wild Talents* (1932), John Keel followed suit. Not everyone in the UFO/paranormal "community" accepts the Fortean and Keelian perspectives but—as ever—the data stand.

Yes, I am familiar with Jacques Vallee's famous statement, "Data is not information..."

If we are ever to learn anything genuine about anomalies, we would do well to heed this snippet from a letter by late UFO-researcher Aimé Michel. To a young Vallee, Michel wrote: "Any progress of the mind consists in gradually stripping away the preconceived ideas, the systems you have inherited. You are right to stir all that up. But do not expect to find the idea that will reassure you, 'the Truth,' if you will. *Above all, Truth means understanding why we don't understand.* Wisdom is to be able to measure what is certain and what is uncertain in science, a fact most so-called 'scientists' are incapable of accomplishing."

Vallee himself eloquently states: "To me, this phenomenon is not simply something that should be investigated, *it is a psychological test*: the first great collective intelligence test to which mankind has been subjected. The sightings put into question both the structure of our society and the laws of our physics. Naturally we are free to run away from this test, as our scientists are currently doing." [2]

Both Michel's and Vallee's statements were written in the mid-1960s. Not only do these exemplify how far advanced and precise in their thoughts these men were, but also how much current mainstream science has resisted change.

Due to the extremely hard work of researchers Donald Hanlon, Jerome Clark, and Lucius Farish there has been found, writes Vallee, "...[A] crucial missing link between the apparitions of older days and modern saucer stories." [3]

"In California, in November, 1896, hundreds of residents of the San Francisco area saw a large, elongated, dark object, which carried brilliant searchlights and was capable of flying against the wind. Between January and March, 1897, it vanished entirely. And suddenly a staggering number of observations of an identical object were made in the Midwest." An earlier report, from one Alexander Hamilton [4], described the craft "...with turbine wheels and a glass section with strange beings aboard looking down...."

"In March, an object of even stranger appearance was seen by Robert Hibbard, a farmer living fifteen miles north of Sioux City, Iowa. Hibbard not only saw the airship, but an anchor hanging from a rope attached to the mysterious craft caught his clothes and dragged him several dozen feet, until he fell back to earth.

"To present in an orderly fashion all the accounts of that period would itself take a book. My object here is only to review the most detailed observations of the behavior of the airship's occupants on the ground. But first, how did the object itself behave? It maneuvered very much in the way UFOs are said to maneuver, except that airships were never seen flying in formation or performing 'aerial dances.' Usually, an airship flew rather slowly and majestically—of course, such an object, in 1897, ran no risk of being pursued—except in a few close-proximity cases when it was reported to depart 'as a shot out of a gun.' Another difference from modern UFOs lies in the fact that its leisurely trajectory often took it over large urban areas. Omaha, Milwaukee, Chicago, and other cities were thus visited; each time, large crowds gathered to watch the object. Otherwise, the airship exhibited all the typical activities of UFOs: hovering, dropping 'probes'—on Newton, Iowa, on April 10, for example—changing course abruptly, changing altitude at great speed, circling, landing and taking off, sweeping the countryside with powerful light beams."

Some landing reports took on aspects of those to come a hundred years hence. "The occupants of the airship were as variously described as are UFO operators. Several reports could be interpreted to mean that dwarfs were among them, but it was not— to my present knowledge, at least—stated in so many words by witnesses....

"All the operators who engaged in discussions with human witnesses were indistinguishable from the average American population of the time. This, for instance, is the experience related by Captain James Hooton (described in the *Arkansas Gazette* as 'the well-known Iron Mountain railroad conductor'): '[while hunting]... As I was tramping through the bush my attention was attracted by a familiar sound, a sound for all the world like the working of an air pump on a locomotive.

"'I went at once in the direction of the sound, and there in an open space of some five or six acres, I saw the object making the noise. To say that I was astonished would but feebly express my feelings. I decided at once that this was the famous airship seen by so many people about the country.

"'There was a medium-size looking man aboard and I noticed that he was wearing smoked glasses. He was tinkering around what seemed to be the back end of the ship, and as I approached I was too dumbfounded to speak. He looked at me in surprise, and said: "Good day, sir; good day." I asked: "Is this the airship?" And he replied: "Yes, sir," whereupon three or four other men came out of what was apparently the keel of the ship.

"'A close examination showed that the keel was divided into two parts, terminating in front like the sharp edge of a knife-like edge, while the side of the ship bulged gradually toward the middle, and then receded. There were three large wheels upon each side made of some bending metal and arranged so that they became concave as they moved forward.

"'I beg your pardon, sir,'I said, 'the noise sounds a great deal like a Westinghouse airbrake.' "'Perhaps it does, my friend: we are using condensed air and aeroplanes, but you will know more later on.'

"'All ready, sir,' someone called out, when the party all disappeared below. I observed that just in front of each wheel a two-inch tube began to spurt air on the wheels and they commenced revolving. The ship gradually arose with a hissing sound. The aeroplanes suddenly sprang forward, turning their sharp end skyward, then the rudders at the end of the ship began to veer to one side and the wheels revolved so fast that one could scarcely see the blades. In less time than it takes to tell you, the ship had gone out of sight."

Apparently "...[Captain Hooton] left a detailed drawing of the machine."

In possibly the most important paragraph of this chapter of Vallee's study, "...[researcher] Jerome Clark observes that 'the 1897 wave indicates the futility of any attempt to divorce flying objects from the general situation in which they operate.' This makes the study of such objects infinitely broader than the simple investigation, in scientific terms, of a new phenomenon; for if the appearance and behavior of the objects are functions of our interpretation at any particular time in the development of our culture, then what chances can we have of ever knowing the truth?"

The next encounter, I must admit, is my favorite in Vallee's book. Why? Because it so clearly illuminates both the intelligence and deception inherent in UFO phenomena.

"March 23, 1966: Temple, Oklahoma. W.E. Laxson, fifty-seven, a civilian instructor with the U.S. Air Force, was driving south toward Sheppard Air Force Base at 5:00 A.M. when he found the road blocked by a large object, the size of a Douglas C-124 Globemaster without wings or engines, resting on pads. A man dressed in coveralls, with a kind of baseball cap on his head, appeared to be examining something on the underside of the craft. When asked how this man looked, Laxson replied:

"'He was just a plain old G.I. mechanic...or a crew chief or whatever he might happen to be on that crew. He had a flashlight in his hand and he was almost kneeling on his right knee with his left hand touching the bottom of the fuselage which was about three feet from the pavement.'

"And he added:

"'People wonder if they looked as "an outer space deal"...I told them I didn't know what "an outer space deal" looked like, but I do know this was made in America, I am sure. It had a plain old G.I. in it, I know that much, I would know the man if I saw him in Chicago tomorrow.'"

Vallee offers what very well might be the most insightful

statement yet formed about UFOs: "What does it all mean? Is it reasonable to draw a parallel between religious apparitions, the fairy-faith, the reports of dwarf-like beings with supernatural powers, the airship tales in the United States in the [1800s], and the present stories of UFO landings?"

NOTES:

1. www.theatlantic.com/technology/archive/2014/06/the-man-who-introduced-the-world-to-flying-saucers/372732/

2. VALLEE, Jacques. *Passport to Magonia: On UFOs, Folklore, and Parallel Worlds* (Contemporary Books, 1969; 1993).

3. Ibid.

4. The Hamilton story proved to be a hoax: http://www.spaceshipsofezekiel.com/html/misc-kansas-airship-cownapping.html

11. BLACK-OPS AND ABDUCTION DECONSTRUCTION

Entering the subject of abduction phenomena is akin to stepping into a hall of well-positioned mirrors.

How can anything as terrifying and apparently otherworldly as abductions be possibly of this world?

Here we descend into very deep, dark waters.

If one absorbs a large dose of the open literature originating in military intelligence, a pattern emerges. As far back as the 1940s, the problem of battle-fatigue was being studied. Compared to the nearly insane pace of present battle-space reality, with much weaponry controlled by computers, World War II seems as if it existed in another continuum.

Today, we have men and women camped in the Nevada deserts operating UAVs (Unmanned Aerial Vehicles), or drones, like the Predator carrying out search-and-destroy missions thousands of miles distant. It is said, even advertised, these operations are similar to playing a very realistic Xbox game. One young drone operator even half-jokingly remarked (paraphrasing here): "All you need is a wide ass and a strong bladder." And, one assumes, some training.

Say what you will, but this does seem to solve many problems inherent in man-to-man recon and combat. However, the very human price of war has yet to be figured. For example, how does one train soldiers to overcome problems such as battle fatigue, endless stress, injury, and remorse over killing? It has been noted elsewhere that today's U.S. soldiers come from mostly "normal" homes (although I could add a *lot* to that opinion).

American kids are, in general, not known to possess the capacity to be ice-blooded killers. True, many can be trained to assume this persona, and to be proficient soldiers—at some cost. Books *have* been written on the topic of what American soldiers face upon returning home from war, little of it pleasant, much of it shameful to a country that considers itself the best.

Hence, the problem at hand: How to make a better soldier. I will admit there are many problems with theories and rumors concerning so-called MILABS—military abductions. Facts are few, but some "alien"-abduction reports contain material pointing in that direction. A MILAB can be loosely described as a scenario wherein a person, or persons, undergo an experience akin to that of so-called alien abductees, except the abductor role is filled by military personnel. Different types of MILABS are reported:

1. The abductee is neutralized by a bright light, often synchronized with a humming, or buzzing, sound. Military personnel—sometimes armed, sometimes not—appear, and escort the target to some vehicle, often a helicopter or van. The abductee may be drugged at this point, possibly to mask any sound or dialogue indicative of the destination. Victims have reported being taken to military appearing installations, normal medical/physicians' offices, and even private homes. [1]

2. The abductee undergoes a "typical" abduction by

otherworldly beings, but once inside the craft encounters a mix of "aliens" and human military personnel. Various vaguely medical procedures are performed, and the victim is returned to the abduction point, or sometimes left in some remote location to fend for him/herself.

Secondary effects—missing time, extreme thirst, panic states, amnesia, burn marks, scars, actinic conjunctivitis—akin to those reported by so-called alien abductees apparently can occur in either of these scenarios.

Researcher/author Helmut Lammer [2], to the best of my knowledge, has done the most in-depth investigation of MILABS, akin to Martin Cannon (although Cannon probably is considered more credible). What Lammer has uncovered, if accurate, is nothing less than shattering.

Lammer quotes a 1996 piece from *New World Vistas*, a military periodical: "In this publication, military scientists suggest that the development of electromagnetic energy sources, the output of which can be pulsed, shaped, and focused and coupled with the human body will be able to: 1) allow one to prevent voluntary muscular movements, 2) control emotions and actions, 3) produce sleep, 4) transmit suggestions, 5) interfere with both short-term and long-term memory, and 6) both produce and delete an experience set [i.e. to simulate a reality]."

According to the late Jim Keith, while military scientists often admit to such experiments, a familiar ploy is one of adding something such as "without much success." This, in an effort to conceal actual progress. Again, such technology (however crude) has existed since at least the 1950s. The real question: who are the test subjects?

As I mentioned in my Introduction, I have no desire to smear the U.S. military or intelligence community. All material in this book comes from open literature, accessible to anyone. While it is not possible to avoid well-placed rumor or speculation, I will always give proper attribution to such material. Few things are more annoying (or money-wasting) than purchasing a book filled with hearsay and cheap shots.

Though not often reported, there are a number of dedicated individuals whose lives have been unnecessarily disrupted (and in some cases ruined) simply because of their interest in anomalous phenomena. It is a fact, however, that a handful of these brave (occasionally foolish) researchers did cross the line between legality and criminal activity. As I noted in my Introduction, I have no "inside" access, nor do I count among my friends and acquaintances ex-intelligence agents. Simply put, I am an omnivorous reader, researcher, and observer. Through decades of activity I have noticed an unforgivable lapse, or tunnel-vision, in more than a few who claim similar pursuits.

Example: well into my 20s I had literally no political interest. The closest I came to that was in paying attention to which presidential candidate might legalize marijuana. Yeah, I know. It's okay to laugh. Certainly my parents did not approve of this stance, but I was genuinely surprised to learn that many of their generation (born around 1920) did think pot should be decriminalized. Funny as it must sound, this got me interested in politics and "how things actually work."

Keep in mind this was well before the Internet, so any material (meaning text) had to be acquired via the library, bookstore, or magazines (primarily, believe it or not, *High Times* and *Rolling Stone*. At the time, these two periodicals published genuine hardcore, even guerrilla, journalism. By that I don't mean every writer was a hero, but certainly many came damned close, such as the late Hunter S. Thompson, William Burroughs, Terry Southern, and even scientists like Terrance Mckenna and his brother Dennis).

I feel honor-bound as a denier of daylight (thank you, Colin Wilson, for coining that monicker!) in claiming that a natural, very human desire to alter my biochemistry, was the genesis of my political awareness.

What I—and doubtless many of my generation—discovered was a much-ignored history of greed, lies, disinformation, corruption, cynical manipulating of official statistics (such as the "body-count" during the Vietnam war and President Nixon, when TV assured us between beer commercials that our enemies were being stacked in mounds), and even conspiracy. Again, go ahead and laugh at our naivety. Again, we had no Internet, cell phones, or their like. We had to think for ourselves in a much (missed) slower, more thoughtful world.

What I came to see, if not understand, was that the world I lived in was not the one my parents inhabited. To them, the "new" world probably felt as chaotic and incomprehensible as present-day reality feels to me. I find it odd that those of my generation rarely discuss how radically different—pre-Internet—were our lives.

Getting back to my contention that some UFO/paranormal researchers sometimes dip their oars into deepest black depths, I am grateful they have done so. It is possible to sift more than a mere few nuggets of fact from these risky adventures. Turn over any large rock and you'll find more than you expected, or even desired.

What I see in present-day publications and Internet data is an apparent mix (dare I say marriage?) of terrorist-financial-ecological crises. A lot of this is hysterical, poorly researched, exploitative, and flat-out crazy. A lot of it is not. Worse, it is nearly impossible, given the vast number of sources, to sift signal from noise. Here is a fictional scenario which demonstrates this notion:

23 OCTOBER 2015: ALIEN INVADERS (OR SOMEBODY) STALK OUR SKIES?
(UPI: Penn Township, PA)
"I promised myself I'd say nothing to anyone about this," says Jeff Stahl, 51, of Jeannette. "But after seeing how many reports were piling up, I thought differently. Why not? A lot of people I know and respect were so upset by what they saw they felt driven to speak up."

Stahl, owner and operator of a local construction firm, shakes his head in ironic regret. "Little did I know," he laughs, "that some arm of our energy commission has aircraft that do not look like conventional stuff—you know, jet airliners, helicopters and so forth. On the other hand, how was I supposed to know this?"

Exactly, as confirmed today by General Edward Lee, Pentagon, as planned: "We do maintain an inventory of unconventional aircraft. Some of these are employed to search for energy assets. Some are used for surveillance. In an explosive world, this is necessary and vital not only to domestic concerns, but to our monitoring of potentially catastrophic climate-change."

(*UFO World* magazine: Winter 2015)
Greetings everyone. Apparently we struck gold, as the

Pennsylvania UFO-sighting reports hit us mere days before sending this issue to press. Your Editor Himself enjoyed a thrilling 46-hour marathon of carpal-tunneling on the ol' keyboard, countless cups of Joe, and much Chinese take-out. You're very welcome.

Before expanding on the sightings and what they might mean, I must give huge thanks to Mr. Timothy Walker of Greensburg, PA, for keeping us constantly updated and providing hundreds of photos and a good amount of video footage (many of these are available on our website).

As most of you are probably aware, a General Edward Lee of the Pentagon (yes, he's an actual person) publicly stated that the sightings were products of human technology. Whether he was happy about this revelation is unknown but, as the photos and especially videos show, this hardly matters. We at *UFO World* like to think we are reasonable, objective, and (mostly) sane— especially when we get more than three hours' sleep. What we have discovered might, if true, be mind-blowing.

I urge you to pass over these words and give close scrutiny to Mr. Walker's astounding photo reproduced on page 19. If you've done this, you will have seen a very clear shot of an unknown aerial vehicle, triangular, gray, and tremendous in size (Mr. Walker did us all great service by taking the photo exactly when he did, at twilight, with the vehicle hovering above a 300-foot tall cellular tower. This is absolutely stunning, better even than the famous [and hoaxed!] "black triangle" allegedly photographed over Belgium in 1990).

In the photo, both the tower and surrounding pines give a reference point to the object's size and altitude. If General Lee planned not to alarm anyone by deploying such a sizable vehicle, I think we can all agree he failed. Too, given the General's own admission that unconventional aircraft are used to suss-out "energy assets" (not to mention for "surveillance"), wouldn't local authority be given warning well ahead of any such activity? Clearly, something stinks in Denmark, and in southwest Pennsylvania, too....

(Postings from various UFO/paranormal websites, late November, early December 2015)
"Do you believe this happy horse-shit?!? I happen to live in

Jeannette, PA, and I'm telling you THERE IS NO "JEFF STAHL"
living here, people. The guy is made up! Even my mother knows
this and she fucking knows EVERYBODY."
  —NiteMan: 2:07A

  "NiteMan U R correct I live there 2! This is a load of
disinformation from BIG BRO!"
  —DeerHunter: 9:20A

"These sound like either the government playing the UFO game or
real UFO's. I don't get it. Why come out and admit THEY were
doing this if they were not?"
  —Becky3: 7:03P

"Jesus H. Christmas you people are nuts. Yes the photos and vids
look real and might very well be, but does that make the craft
extraterrestrial? Hell NO in my book. This is EXACTLY the kind
of stuff—black-ops, etc,—Jim Keith warned us about before they
snuffed him. WAKE UP!"
  —Patriot4Eagle: 12:11A
  I employed the above fictional scenario to show how

reactionary the UFO/Paranormal "community" can be.

  While I will never "force" anyone to trust me, my fictional

indulgence—like bad booze—is actually quite watered down.

"Real life" contains content far more vicious, insane, and

combustible.

  Why? Belief systems (our old enemy) taint practically all fields

of investigation, nowhere more visibly than on the Internet; and

believers in extraterrestrials are as fervent—and irrational—as

religious fundamentalists. Anyone who doubts this need only

disagree with a hardcore believer. Now, on the other hand, don't

use my example to actually start trouble! I reviewed tonight one

meager example of emotional tinder, a video-clip I'll title "Very

Shocking Haunting." I'd like to claim I'm old-hat at picking out shit from rubies regarding any film/video footage of so-called anomalous phenomena, and stand by this claim.

The title (very close to my protect-the-guilty fake) itself set me up for laughs and some amount of anger. Three little girls sitting atop a bed giggling and playing, when abruptly the bed starts rocking and jumping. The girls look only somewhat shocked, then explode into absolutely the worst acting I've ever witnessed beyond *Plan 9 From Outer Space*. At least until their brave daddy bursts into the room and saves them.

Anyone reading this knows there are hundreds, if not thousands, of videos similar to this. Most appear as if their makers just slogged down their last Monster or Red Bull, wiped pizza grease from shaky hands, and powered off the DVD player after a session of *Paranormal Activity*, or *The Blair Witch Project*. This is reprehensible behavior. What, in their few moments of sustained attention, can such people be thinking?

Please understand I'd love to provide the actual information to these, but cannot afford lawsuits. My favorite, most despised, was a home video shot by two pre-teen boys, and involving Mothman. Thank God their ineptly spelled header *warned* me I might be disturbed by the footage—I was.

I must (dammit!) paraphrase the shaky, ingenuous voice-over: "Like, me and my brother were playing Guitar Hero and, like, saw something in our backyard. You won't believe it, but it was Mothman!"

This came close in me to inducing vomiting, but, God bless

them, the boys were way ahead of me. Stepping onto the deck of his parents' luxurious home, one boy shouts, "There it is!" The shaky-cam tries, and fails, to focus on two red points of light, when our boy abruptly bends at the waist and vomits on the deck. Screaming, he dashes into the kitchen and does this again over dishes stacked in the sink. The family dog saunters into the room, and our boy wipes his mouth and shakes his head. The End.

Why am I wasting space relating these sorry ventures? Because, even though it may sound as if I'm killing flies with atom bombs, the matter is more serious. Worshipers of the Internet and All Things Digital will hate me, but I don't care. Yes, my examples were produced by children (and their parents) and *probably* were not intended to cause alarm. I have tried to imagine myself, at the age of 10 or thereabouts, armed with digital tech. Would I have done the same? I can't be sure, but it is possible.

What I *am* sure of is that such kids are nowhere near as naive as I was at their age, and *meant* to "get a rise" out of clueless viewers, or gain some obscure form of "fame." What they do *not* know is how reckless they are in so doing. They add fuel to the fire of those who consider anything involving UFOs/paranormal phenomena as purest bullshit. There are countless examples produced by others more "adult." They all stink.

As anyone reading this knows, photographs and videos of anomalous phenomena are very easy to fabricate, in a way not possible even as little as 10 years ago. This burden is destructive and absolutely unnecessary to serious investigators.

Sometimes I wonder why anyone still thinks they need to put

blame on world governments for producing disinformation. We seem to be doing this just fine without them. Worse, those mishandling their apparently endless free time often consider hoaxing as "creative" and funny. Right. These clueless idiots are no different from Guitar Hero players who, simply because they have mastered a few songs, believe they're ready to jump on stage with Bad Religion (I have enjoyed the game myself, but understand the vast difference between virtual and genuine!).

I'm sure I'm not alone in my assessment of the Internet as both blessing and curse. True, it *is* an amazing tool. Sadly, far too many users can find nothing better to do with such freedom than use it as a juvenile playground. Decades ago TV was accused of the same, but that does not hold true for the Internet: TV-watching was—always will be—a passive experience. Our little hoaxers on the Net do not realize they are freely assisting Those in High Places hiding genuinely dangerous material, much of which has nothing whatsoever to do with UFOs and paranormal phenomena.

NOTES:

1. CANNON, Martin. *The Controllers: A New Hypothesis of "Alien" Abductions.* www.bibliotecapleyades.net/sociopolitica/esp_sociopol_mindcon04.htm

2. http://kymufon.anomalyresponse.org/helmut.html

12. PERSONAL ANOMALIES

In summer 1992 I was employed by a high-tech firm that manufactured test-and-measurement instruments for university labs, computer firms, and defense contractors. My job entailed data-processing and the nightly back-up of the company's files on the HP-3000 mainframe. At that time we still used large tape spools, each requiring about an hour to fill. My routine was to insert the first tape, then head out to grab a sandwich to be eaten in the computer room. One night as I was driving back to the site (which probably prefers not to be named), I noticed on my left beneath heavy cloud cover two large, glaring white lights. As an amateur astronomer and fan of all things that fly, I possess good skills at identifying just about anything one might observe in the sky.

The lights were separated by perhaps two or three hundred feet, and at first I thought they were independent of each other. They drifted slowly, much more so than any aircraft. I turned onto the long drive that lead to the site, stopped my car and stepped out into a light drizzle. As the lights passed overhead (at an estimated altitude of 1,000 feet) I could see they were not in fact separate, but were attached to some dark, long object. Abruptly, the lights halted, then rotated until they were vertically placed. Beyond the warm drizzle, no sound could be heard. *A blimp,* I told myself. *Has to be*. After all, the firm was located not more than 30 miles north of Akron, Ohio, home to the Goodyear blimp, fixture of many sports events in nearby Cleveland and elsewhere.

What I did not know was that dirigibles usually don't fly at night. But even if they did, surely there would be the familiar buzzing drone of engines.

All at once cold fear surged through me. *I'm looking at a UFO...an old-school cigar-shaped UFO!*

Now I understood what witnesses to the unknown meant when they described being "riveted in place."

My heart hammered. The lights slowly, hypnotically, ascended into the clouds and vanished.

After a few moments of light panic, I climbed into my car and drove down the dark, pine-walled drive to the company lot.

Inside, I wrote in my ever-present journal what I'd witnessed while it was still fresh and alive in my mind. Eating my sandwich I noticed I could not stop my hands from shaking, and feared being alone. What had I seen? Had it been a genuine UFO? Certainly I was unable to identify the object.

For what it's worth, there was nothing in my system stronger than coffee and pastrami.

My point here is that the first thought I had was that *I saw a UFO*. Simply, an unidentified flying object. My fear is evidence that I immediately assumed the thing had to be extraterrestrial, even though, in my intellectual arrogance, I should have known better. But I didn't. At home later, I took personal inventory. No "missing time." No secondary physical effects such as extreme thirst, burning eyes, or feelings of unreality.

Caught up in my fear (and, perhaps, desire to see a UFO), I had abandoned all objective reasoning.

Not many people know that military technology is approximately 15 years ahead of what the Department of Defense allows us to see, and read about in the open literature. Classified, "black-ops" aircraft often are tested at night. However, as investigator Stan Gordon mentioned to me during a telephone conversation (regarding the huge, triangular UFOs written about by himself and, most prominently, Philip Imbrogno in his *Night Siege: the Hudson Valley UFO Sightings*) [1], it is illegal to operate classified aircraft over populated zones; though I'm fairly certain this "rule" once in a while is ignored. (On a side note, I am aware that Philip Imbrogno apparently has left the "field," after accusations of dishonesty regarding facts of his military service and education. Whether Imbrogno faked a few credits is none of my business, and personally I don't see how, even if true, such regrettable behavior bears on his published material. I do think, however, that in a few of his investigations—notably the "demon" voice and sounds he claimed to have tape-recorded in 1978 [2]— he could have dug deeper. New to research, though, and much younger, he might have lacked resources.)

So, *what* did I see?

My guess is that the object was not a classified aircraft and thus illegal. Despite what my readers might think, I do not believe any arm of American defense is reckless enough to risk a potential catastrophe—human and legal—by flying whatever UFO-like vehicles in their arsenal over our cities.

Therefore, what I saw either was some very large blimp-like craft or...something else.

And I behaved poorly by losing myself to self-indulgent paranoia and fear. Had I kept my wits, who knows what I might have seen. Perhaps something more prosaic than a UFO.

Another, much earlier, incident might have been my first experience of a waking dream, or hypnopompic imagery—though it didn't (as most claim) "feel" at all dream-like. This, of course, doesn't prove anything. As John Keel noted in *Operation Trojan Horse* [3]: "This type of vision is well known to students of psychic phenomena. The immobility or akinesia...is especially common in the 'bedroom visitant' cases in which percipients awaken to sense or even see an intruder in their bedroom—an intruder who melts away after passing along a message or a warning. Psychiatrists tend to dismiss this type of phenomenon as hypnopompic; that is, the vision is thought to be a dream that overlaps into the waking state."

My experience occurred several years before the "cryptid" sighting I described in Chapter 1, probably 1965. I woke one morning and saw a figure in a long white garment standing with its back to me, leaning over the shelf displaying my collection of plastic model airplanes. I had the impression this intruder held one of my works, and was closely examining it—then I knew! It had to be my sister, snooping around in her nightgown. I reached for her back, and my hand sank into her as if into fog. I cried out...

That's the extent of my memory. There was no akinesia, or sleep paralysis.

Like my later incident with the strange "bird," the memory is visually textured with absolute, dead-pan realism. The sun was up, my room bright enough for me to distinguish a solid object from a phantom...for all the good it did in the long-view.

What bothers me, probably as much as not knowing with certainty the source of these experiences, is that many, many others have similar encounters somewhere every day...and due to personal belief systems lock onto one perspective—for all their lives. I cannot say that about myself, can I? I'm open to several theories regarding my three.

Beyond these, there have been a handful of "meandering nocturnal lights" too vague to draw any conclusions about, and one striking daylight sighting (with my mother, father, and sister around 1980 driving near Circleville, Ohio, on our way to a cabin at Burr Oak State Park). I have some confusion about the exact date, which may have been earlier, possibly 1978 or 1979. My father had pulled the car off the highway, whether in response to some feared malfunction, or in response to one of us pointing out the object in the cloudless autumn sky. We climbed out, and stood watching a round (as in spherical) object, of some transparent material moving about as fast as a small single-engine airplane. This might have been a balloon, either very large and high, or small and much lower than we thought. What gives the sighting a lingering strangeness to me is the smooth, precise flight of the object. Balloons, weather and otherwise—bob and pause and react to upper (and lower) winds. I have searched MUFON and other files for reports, but with no success (no surprise there, as fewer than 10% of all UFO sightings ever are reported).

I suppose I do have faith of a kind: that there is more in the multiverse than us. I cannot remember who said, regarding the possibility that if humankind is alone, that it would be an awful waste of space...I agree.

We possess the greatest set of tools to explore these ultimate mysteries, but I think we confuse the tools with the house. In other words, science, logic, theory, and philosophy can take us only so far. Of course we must never abandon these, but must imagine something beyond, something never before thought or visualized.

Our world needs, for lack of a better term, an Einstein of the soul, of creative consciousness. It is my contention that truly great minds need not be hijacked into weapons production, economic theory and control, or the ever-shattering hall of mirrors we call politics. These are little more than symptoms of a civilization dangerously, tragically, falling apart.

The "truth" of our existence might very well turn out to be that in order to survive we must be smart enough to defeat our animal impulses, something we are still very far away from achieving.

I'd like to think that we simply have lost our breath in the long, agonizing climb up the ladder of evolution; that our current miseries *can* be overcome so long as enough of us dare to gaze into infinity with care and wonder and joy that we are here at all.

There are those who say humankind requires both "good" and "evil," or the more secular "positive" and "negative" in perpetuity to maintain a tension between progress and apathy. Though not a fan of the terminology, I think I agree with this notion of balance. It is, after all, a fact in most physical processes—from those of galactic scale, down to quantum foam....

If I've gained anything lasting from decades of reading, occasionally investigating, and spending hours thinking about the unknown behind life, it is this: we are not alone. Whether products of blind evolution or intelligent design, I don't know. But I urge you to beware of anyone claiming to possess the answers to humankind's deepest mystery. No one has that answer—not even religion, tomes cobbled together by (mostly) well-meaning scribes, limited by being born into a culture and time beyond their control. As am I. One hundred years (assuming Earth's survival) from now, these words might very well sound as silly as do those now from the 15th century. If so, that could be only a sign of progress, or (pessimistically) ignorance of history. Collectively, humankind's record for learning from what has come before is not good.

We fail still to learn that technological progress outpaces the spiritual, meat and blood, reality of our lives. A sad fact, but one we seem incapable of transcending. History has shown, again and again, that not all progress is for the better. Our increasing loneliness among black cradling gulfs gets no easier to bear, and the only "answers" seem to come from soulless exploiters interested only in their own future.

It's hard to endure an existence without a received meaning. I think the only meaning possible in life is that with which we invest it. Those with faith do not have this burden, but others—like me— certainly do. And it's no good imploring—no matter how much I appreciate the gesture—me to get along with religion. Any "intellectual" will say the same. You can't "unknow" what you've learned—at least I can't. Often I wish I could, but that would be dishonest and disrespectful—to me *and* you.

It ought to be "enough" for me to accept the mysteries of life— but it isn't. This, in my mind, points toward a survival instinct. Without some unbalance, progress withers. In nature, and in humankind. Of this—despite its collective pain—I am certain. And it really hurts—as you know. We don't get to choose our hurts. A poignant line from Mark Pellington's *Mothman Prophecies* assures us: "We aren't allowed to know..."

Life is strange.

Choosing not to explore it would be stranger still.

Here's to exploration...and discovery.

Depressing as it sounds, I am liberated by Jacques Vallee's contention that it doesn't matter whether UFOs are "real" physical machines. How could it? What *does* matter is their psychosocial effect on very real human beings. Vallee was right in stating that everyone knows about Jesus Christ, but no one can prove he actually existed. Again, that doesn't matter. Billions of living souls believe in his "message," and the example of his teachings. The ultimate psychosocial effect—and not a bad one at that. The UFO "phenomenon," whatever its source, wields similar power—for good or ill. And that is what we ought to study—not physical evidence, forever 10 steps ahead of us like the fairy games of time immemorial.

I'd be remiss not to admit I'm a fairly "passionate" follower of post-post modern conspiracy theory, much of which never comes close to "theory." We have plenty of rants, raves, and snarling vows of vengeance. Stone-cold revelations whispered in dark holdouts haunted by suicide; reason and safety stalked by black dogs of paranoia sniffing for logic-bombs. Nightly, the star-frosted sky thrums with machines stabbing down beams aggressively intelligent; watching and watching with infrared eyes. Thermal tongues lapping up secrets. Waiting...waiting...infinitely patient. Scanning thoughts for a nanosecond glitch in your vigilance—your blazing annihilation.

If that doesn't make you feel better, nothing will. Even a cursory cruise of a few "edgy" websites will provide a representative slice of what the more pensive observers are saying about the apparently enigmatic fate of Flight 370. These remarks range from straight, journalistic-type reportage, to chilly monographs grim with doubt; flat recounting of the original report, and what I am now calling NFM: Nefarious Fear-Mongering. While I'm not sure who started this, a famous "alien abductee" is hinting that Flight 370 might very well have been sky-jacked and safely landed on dry ground in some remote location. While he doesn't clearly explain what might have been done to the 239 people occupying the aircraft, he theorizes it might be used by terrorists, and capable of delivering a 10,000-pound nuclear device to any major city within 12,000 miles.

This might be technically possible, if not probable. But it is a theory—an outlandish one. A little research into how weapons-grade plutonium is acquired, and processed, will put such notions to rest. What I *am* confused about is the—at least to my mind—inexplicable failure to locate the aircraft's Black Box. Media reports claim signals have been detected, but finding the actual site (so far) impossible. Why? We have classified satellites that can identify earthbound individuals, and more. The NSA, by 2018, hopes to have a computer capable of exaflop speed—1,000,000,000,000,000,000 operations a second. That's one quintillion [4]. Yes, data-collection is one thing; taking time to interpret said data quite another. The Black Box (actually, these are orange for easier detection) is fitted with an Underwater Locator Beacon functional down to 14,000 feet—nearly three miles. The devices have been heat-tested, withstanding 1,110 degrees centigrade for an hour; 260-degree C for 10 hours. They can operate between -55 degrees to +70 degrees C. Seriously tough hardware. If a signal has been detected, and if every signal has a *source*, why can't the Black Box be located?

NOTES:

1. HYNEK, Dr. J. Allen; IMBROGNO, Philip J.; and PRATT, Bob. *Night Siege: The Hudson Valley UFO Sightings* (Llewellyn Publications expanded edition, 1998).

2. IMBROGNO, Philip J. *Interdimensional Universe: The New Science of UFOs, Paranormal Phenomena & Otherdimensional Beings* (Llewellyn Publications, 2008).

3. KEEL, John. *Operation Trojan Horse* (Manor Books, Inc. 1970; Anomalist Books edition 2013).

4. BAMFORD, James. *The Shadow Factory: The Ultra-Secret NSA from 9/11 to the Eavesdropping on America* (Doubleday, 2008).

13. THINKING CLEARLY ABOUT MIND CONTROL

I considered not writing about the disputatious topic of mind control, as much of the more questionable material I've studied came from that end of the high-strangeness spectrum. Earlier this year, however, I reviewed the entire text of the August 3, 1977 *Project MKULTRA, The CIA's Program of Research in Behavioral Modification Joint Hearing Before the Select Committee on Intelligence.* [1]

Finely put together by the venerable U.S. Government Printing Office, this document is all anyone could conceivably require in order to be convinced of the reality of such nefarious projects in history and—perhaps—present day.

Now, with six weeks before this book's publication, I have "secured" and re-read a copy of what many consider *the* masterwork...Walter Bowart's *Operation Mind Control* [2]. Among the most disturbing, unpleasant books I've ever read, *OMC* is nonetheless fascinating, and more riveting than any literary or cinematic thriller could ever hope to be (many of these scoured Bowart's book for material). It's easy for any reader to see how this book stocked—in 1979—the conspiracy buffet of JFK assassination theories. With a difference. Bowart's theories actually are plausible, and stand mostly apart from others. It has been established that many of those involved in the Warren

Commission report eventually disowned it, and with good reason. For all the so-called investigation into the event, some basic evidence was amazingly ignored.

The combined impact of these works convinced me to include a chapter on mind control, and I'm convinced that no serious—or even semi-serious—researcher and/or writer of anomalous aerial phenomena and associated activity can with integrity ignore (no matter how tempting) this exceedingly dark topic. Unlike so much else covered here, hard evidence—*proof* if you will—exists to support the grim reality of behavioral modification programs used against unwitting, unwilling human subjects. Like Walter Bowart, I absolutely endorse "...an exercise in citizens' intelligence...the need for informed discretion in a democracy."

Yet a third lengthy document joins those mentioned above; one aware of both, and what I consider the third in an unacknowledged mind-control "trilogy": Martin Cannon's *The Controllers*. [3]

First, though, I'm honor-bound to mention that Cannon has apparently disavowed his thesis, which originally was published as a long paper, and in 1996 a thick book by Feral House. In both works, Cannon's subtitle is *A New Hypothesis of Alien Abductions*. Second, Martin Cannon no longer contributes material to, or commentary on, anything associated with Ufology. The usual rumors are out there, and I bypassed them to write an article seen by many readers, wherein I asked if anyone could enlighten me on the status of Mr. Cannon. To date, I've received not a single response.

Ominous? Perhaps. But I doubt it. Cannon wouldn't be the first, or the last, to turn away in disgust from the Ufology "community" if in fact that's what transpired.

For our purposes in this chapter, though, we will explore at some length an article Cannon wrote for the premiere issue (Summer 1994) of *The Anomalist*: "The Numbers Game." While Cannon's *The Controllers* digs deep into mind-control lore—much of it documented—his semi-autobiographical *Anomalist* piece might very well have illuminated a telling aspect of mind-control operations, and why this particular process might have been employed beginning in the early 1960s.

Anyone reading this book is liable to have heard about the enigmatic "number-reading" and "rapid-fire foreign language" telephone intrusions reported to John Keel in *The Mothman Prophecies*. Cannon's "The Numbers Game" shares his own experiences, which occurred during "the Reagan years"—proving the process (whatever its ultimate purpose) was active from at least 1961 (Keel's first mention of a case in Oregon) through the early 1980s. Whatever the process, it must have been effective to remain —according to reports—essentially unchanged for over two decades.

The article opens with Cannon's mentioning he occasionally writes about UFOs, and once in a while:

...someone will ask me: "Has anything weird ever happened to you?"
I always reply "No." But that's not quite true. I can bear witness to one minor but maddening enigma—one which veteran outer-limits researcher John Keel (and a very few other authors) connect to the UFO controversy.
In *The Mothman Prophecies,* Keel writes of a United Nations

public relations officer named Don Estrella, who survived a head-on automotive encounter with an invisible, impenetrable something-or-other that accordioned the front end of his car. Shortly after this bizarre accident, a friend of Estrella's in Long Island received an odd phone call. The U.N. officer reported that, "A voice that sounded very distant said 'Hello, Don.' My friend told him that I hadn't arrived yet. The voice then began to recite a series of numbers meaninglessly."

Keel knew of many similar incidents. In 1961, a telephone conversation between two women in Oregon was rudely interrupted by the voice of a mysterious man who shouted "Wake up down there!" According to Keel, "The voice started to rattle on in a rapid-fire language that sounded like Spanish." After this odd locution ceased, the women could speak together normally once more. At the same time next day, the women spoke on the phone again, only to ear-witness a repeat performance by the oddball voice. After the audio interloper speed-shouted something in a foreign tongue, it began reciting the numbers forty and twenty-five continually...

In 1967, during West Virginia's great "Mothman" wave of UFO-oriented oddities, Keel encountered the phenomenon again. Every night, a young lady in the area was called by a strange man who would speak to her in an accelerated speech that sounded "something like Spanish...yet I don't think it is Spanish."

Now, to paraphrase an old Bill Cosby line, I told you those stories to tell you this one.

Because, you see, it happened to me.

Cannon then describes his personal circumstances: crummy apartment, bad graveyard-shift jobs which on nights off resulted in boredom:

My brother suggested loop lines.

He had learned of these from a computer bulletin board...

The telephone company invented loops to serve some arcane testing purpose which need not concern us here. The important point is that 99.9999% of the time the lines lie dormant—officially. Unofficially, they're a phreak phantasia. Imagine phone lines connected to no telephone, lines that "float" somewhere in the central office of the Telco (if you'll forgive the lapse into phreak-speak). Loops come in matched pairs, and the numbers usually occur in the upper strata of an exchange. Thus, if you dial (212) XXX-9977, you'll speak to whoever might be waiting on (212) XXX-9978.

Why do this? Basically, it's networking for nerds: The loops serve as a sort of lonely-heart's club, whereby individuals in widely separated cities can compare notes in the safety of telephonic anonymity. Occasionally, opposite-sex phreaks loop into each other, resulting in long-distance romances...by using loops one could "avoid long-distance charges." In other words: free calls. Phreak samsara...

Then I heard The Voice.

Actually, The Voice was preceded by The Tone, a subtle electric buzz somewhat akin to the sound you hear when you hold a seashell to your ear. This faded away, gradually replaced by a young, male Voice reading numbers.

"27...28...29...27...28...29...27..."

As I recall, the numbers never dipped below 20 or above 60. The Voice did not acknowledge anything I said to it. Was it a machine? Perhaps—although this was no simple tape loop. Every so often, the voice would interrupt its strange soliloquy and shout:

"Wake up out there!"

Then more numbers. (Keel's informants recall the statement as "Wake up down there!" Since I never achieved a clear-as-a-bell connection, I suppose either reading is possible.)

More rarely, I heard gibberish sessions—the odd, sped-up instructions in a strangely familiar foreign language...

I had to know what was going on.

Thereafter, whenever the gods of loopdom connected me with a seasoned phone phreak, I would inquire about the "Number-Man." After all, the Telco used loops to test new exchanges; wasn't it possible that these strange monologues constituted some part of the test?

Negative, the experts told me...

Had other phreaks also heard these strange messages? A few had. They were just as puzzled as I. Moreover, the telephone company couldn't provide any official explanation—it doesn't even like to admit that loop lines exist. So if anyone was going to solve the enigma, it had to be me.

At this point, Cannon manages to tape-record the Number Man, producing a "greatest hits" cassette that unfortunately no longer exists. This admission, from so staunch an investigator, is hard for me to take—I would have copied the cassette, sealed the original, and locked it away in a safe-deposit box.

Events turned yet more mysterious:

One night shortly thereafter, following a few unsuccessful encounters with my numerically-obsessed nemesis, I looped into someone even more interesting—who, I now suspect, may also have played a role in this enigmatic drama. Her name was Joanne, and her voice was so agonizingly sexy I felt tempted to propose to her the moment she whispered my name.

Joanne claimed to be a stripper living in Montreal, and turned up the flame yet more by telling Cannon she wanted to meet with him. After more back-and-forth, Joanne told him she *knew* he was better and smarter than the men she encountered as a stripper. To his credit, Cannon admits alarms were ringing in the back of his lonely mind, validated when the too-good-to-be-true woman asked him to write a letter describing everything about his life. She provided an address. But Cannon, wisely, never took the next step:

Nearly a decade later, Joanne's (admittedly delightful) intrusion strikes me as deeply mystifying. Was she really just a lonely ecdysiast? Perhaps—but there was something oddly theatrical about the episode, which seemed designed to fulfill every aspect of a lonely-guy's most outlandish fantasy. Joanne was too good. Was I really so charming a fellow that this pretty young thing felt compelled to meet me after I had burped out no more than a hazy half-sentence or two?

One thing's for sure: She almost received a great deal of information about me.

Maybe that was the point...

And yet: I don't think the answer lies with UFOs. I think we're dealing with spies.

I had never heard the Spy Theory before reading it in Cannon's evocative article, but the more I thought about it the more sensible the notion became.

Cannon goes on to mention William Poundstone's book *Big Secrets* [4], wherein the author wonders whether the number-reading and sped-up voices might be codes used by drug-runners. Poundstone later reported, on tabloid TV program *Eye on L.A.*, how some victimized short-wave enthusiasts had "triangulated the broadcasts to their most probable origin point: The state of Virginia. Which pretty much gives the game away."

Cannon continues by explaining that the rapid-fire voices might be "screech" broadcasts—sped-up in order to guarantee incomprehensibility if intercepted by the wrong ears. The message is decoded by recording it, and replaying at a slower speed. Cannon wonders whether the flirtatious woman he spoke with might have been a ploy to ferret out useful intelligence from someone who had inadvertently discovered the operation.

The article so far has done a superb job of laying down reasonable "explanations" for the enigma, except for coming to grips with an annoying fact: the apparent randomness of the telephone calls. Cannon thinks some of these might be used to induce telephonic trance, something many researchers in hypnosis do not take seriously. These researchers are wrong.

Released CIA documents from projects ARTICHOKE, BLUEBIRD, MKULTRA—the obscure paper-trail of the mind-controllers—tell a different story (findable in Bowart's aforementioned *Operation Mind Control*). One document "unequivocally asserts that telephonic induction of a deep hypnotic trance was successfully tested in the early 1950s." Cannon notes that John Keel, in *The Mothman Prophecies*, *Operation Trojan Horse* [5] and others (probably he meant *The Eighth Tower*), strongly affirms that "selected" UFO witnesses seem to be affected by some form of posthypnotic suggestion.

This is a troubling thread weaving through Ufology and even what appear to be "prosaic" phenomena such as hauntings and poltergeist reports, to say nothing of documented official projects to create mind-controlled "sleeper" agents and assassins.

From all accounts, sometimes our minds actually are *not* our own....

NOTES:

1.www.nytimes.com/packages/pdf/national/13inmate_ProjectMKULTRA.pdf

2. BOWART, Walter. *Operation Mind Control* (Dell Publishing Co., Inc. 1978).

3. CANNON, Martin. *The Controllers: A New Hypothesis of "Alien" Abductions*. www.bibliotecapleyades.net/sociopolitica/esp_sociopol_mindcon04.htm

4. POUNDSTONE, William. *Big Secrets* (William Morrow and Company, Inc. 1983).

5. KEEL, John. *Operation Trojan Horse* (Manor Books, Inc. 1970; Anomalist Books edition 2013).

14. COLIN WILSON'S *THE OUTSIDER* AND *POLTERGEIST!: A STUDY IN DESTRUCTIVE HAUNTING*

Colin Wilson passed away on December 5, 2013, leaving behind what amounts to a small library of works exploring existential philosophy, the paranormal, UFOs, crime, sexuality, wine, poetry, books, writing, Hermann Hesse, Rasputin, film-director Ken Russell, and more—that's the nonfiction list. He also wrote a number of novels based on his investigations and research, the best known of which is probably *The Space Vampires* (1976), filmed by Tobe Hooper as *Lifeforce* in 1985.

But it is his first book, *The Outsider* (1956) [1], that simultaneously deconstructed philosophy and offered a new direction of stunning insight and brilliance. Wilson was 24, and had been sleeping out on Hampstead Heath to save money. He quickly became loved and loathed in equal measure, and was crowned one of England's "Angry Young Men," a title he did not like.

The Outsider was—is still—the seminal work on "alienation, creativity, and the modern mind-set." Wilson defined the Outsider as "[A] man who has awakened to chaos... For the Outsider, the world is not rational, not orderly. When he asserts his sense of anarchy in the face of the bourgeois' complacent acceptance, it is not simply the need to cock a snook at respectability that provokes

him; it is a distressing sense *that truth must be told at all costs*,
otherwise there can be no hope for an ultimate restoration of order.
'He sees too deep and too much.'...."

Colin Wilson certainly did, and as a teenager came within
minutes of suicide before realizing the utter absurdity and self-pity
of the notion.

He dug into the lives and works of Kafka, Camus, Eliot,
Hemingway, Van Gogh, Nietzsche, Dostoyevsky, Rimbaud and
others, exemplars of the Outsider psyche. What made them tick?
Why did most of them come to such dismal ends?

Wilson concluded that what the overcomplicated world needs is
a new religion—based in neo-existentialism powered by
imagination and increasing the intentionality, or "pressure," of
consciousness. He saw the Outsider as society's spiritual/creative
dynamo, whose intellectual and artistic works inspire the masses
into a higher sense of purpose. Without them, there would be no
progress.

***

With *Poltergeist!: A Study in Destructive Haunting* (1981) [2],
Wilson utilized decades of study and research to explore one of the
world's most violent, provocative, and baffling mysteries.

Wilson was fascinated by the power exhibited in many
poltergeist manifestations—they could easily kill, but seemed not
to like being around people. And how could they pound against a
house with what sounded like a wrecking ball, yet cause no
vibration or damage? They did, however, cause considerable
damage to the home and belongings of the Pritchard family in

Pontefract, an ancient English market town in West Yorkshire.

Wilson chronicles the chaos, which began with the family finding inexplicable puddles of water in the house. Soft rapping noises followed. Neighbors blamed the Pritchard's children, but since they were present during much of the activity, had to be ruled out.

At one point an egg floated into the living room, and violently exploded—saturating the space with an overpowering aroma of flowers. Mr. and Mrs. Pritchard witnessed in their daughter's bedroom part of a wooden window frame ripped out and smashed through the window. It had been secured with two-inch screws. Whenever someone came over to the house and made critical remarks suggesting the outbreak was explainable without invoking the supernatural, Mr. Nobody (as the poltergeist came to be named) reacted violently—hurling a grandfather clock down stairs where it exploded like a bomb on the landing, and doing the same to the hall stand (a very heavy piece of furniture), except this time floating it until it pressed the Pritchard's daughter Diane against the stairs, which could have crushed her to death.

Wilson thought the poltergeist "possessed his own juvenile and rather destructive sense of humor," and seemed provoked by Mrs. Pritchard's tidiness (which it proved by unspooling toilet paper and smearing door handles and the staircase with mustard, jam, and marmalade). When mention was made of bringing a priest into the house, Mr. Nobody demonstrated anti-Christian sentiments by pulling a brass crucifix from the wall and forcing it against Diane's back. No one could remove it—as if the girl had become magnetized. She panicked and the cross fell off, leaving an angry cross-shaped welt between her shoulder blades. When the family returned home from an Easter Sunday outing, they found gold crosses painted on doors, detailed as if from a stencil and spray can. They were unable to duplicate this, as the paint wouldn't adhere to the doors' polished surfaces.

Eventually the activity dwindled, then ended, as most so-called poltergeist outbreaks do. Wilson theorized that some kind of bored elemental spirits are attracted to unhappy homes, and use that energy to perform their amazing feats. It was a fact that Joe Pritchard—a sports enthusiast—did not get along with his son, who preferred books and music.

Wilson became aware of the work of Dr. J.L. Whitton, who had done laboratory analyses of recordings of "spirit raps," found them very different in quality than normal percussive sounds. On a graph, ordinary sound signatures curve, rising and falling like a mountain. Poltergeist noise begins abruptly and ends the same way. They seemed not to bother dogs, who, if they noticed the sounds at all seemed to perceive them as nonthreatening.

Later, Wilson listened to the rarest of poltergeist phenomena: voices. The investigator/author Guy Playfair [3] had recordings of a particularly aggressive spirit—or something. "When Guy Playfair asked: 'Do you know you are dead?' the voice said angrily: *'Shut up!'* And to further requests that it go away, it replied: *"Fuck off."* Wilson and Playfair noted the masculine growl had an odd electronic quality, parsed as if each word were formed separately.

Finally, Wilson concludes that poltergeists might actually be semi-intelligent energy fields that feed from the "leaking energies" of distressed people, and seem to possess control over matter, able to pass solid objects through other solid surfaces in the form of "apports." These can be anything, but usually are coins, keys, stones, and small personal items.

Wilson wonders at the malice of the forces, and that they're apparently limited, perhaps by some unknown "law" of physics. And, finally, "[W]here evil is concerned, human beings have a monopoly."

NOTES:

1. WILSON, Colin. *The Outsider* (Victor Gollancz Ltd., 1956; Jeremy P. Tarcher, Inc., 1982).

2. _____. *Poltergeist!: A Study in Destructive Haunting* (New York: Putnam, 1981; Llewellyn edition, 1993).

3. PLAYFAIR, Guy. *The Indefinite Boundary: An Investigation into the Relationship between Matter and Spirit* (London: Souvenir Press, 1980).

15. THE PENTACLE MEMORANDUM AND PROJECT STORK—(UFO) GAME OVER?

Because of the explosive material contained in this Battelle Memorial Institute document, I'm reproducing the entire text. It was discovered by Jacques Vallee [1] on June 18, 1967, while he was organizing J. Allen Hynek's UFO files. Vallee admits the document intimidated him: "[W]hat these people were recommending was nothing less than a carefully calibrated and monitored simulation of an entire UFO wave." He struggled over telling Hynek about finding the memo, and in September 1968 he inserted it between a reproduction of *The Lady and the Unicorn* tapestry and the frame's cardboard before leaving for France.

Once overseas, he told Hynek about the memo.

Angry and worried, Hynek went to Columbus and confronted "Pentacle" and his team at Battelle—and had his notes plucked from his hands. Hynek, known for his awe of secrecy and occasional timidness, wanted to go public but feared the results. Pentacle, aware of this, was careful not to fire Hynek (who was at the time consulting for Project Blue Book), but created the Condon Report which made Hynek's position with ATIC (Air Technical Intelligence Center) at Wright-Patterson Air Force Base redundant.

Whether the simulation of UFO waves ever was put into action cannot be known, but there exists plenty of evidence that it was—

the incredible Point Pleasant activity, for one.

SECRET
SECURITY INFORMATION

G-1579-4

cc: B. D. Thomas
H. C. Cross/A. D. Westerman
L. R. Jackson
W. T. Reid
P. J. Rieppal
V. W. Ellsey/R. J. Lund January 9, 1953
Files
Extra [handwritten]

Mr. Miles E. Coll
Box 9575
Wright-Patterson Air Force Base, Ohio

Attention Capt. Edward J. Ruppelt

Dear Mr. Coll:
This letter concerns a preliminary recommendation to ATIC on future methods of handling the problem of unidentified aerial objects. This recommendation is based on our experience to date in analyzing several thousands of reports on this subject. We regard the recommendation as preliminary because our analysis is not yet complete, and we are not able to document it where we feel it should be supported by facts from the analysis.

We are making this recommendation prematurely because of a CIA-sponsored meeting of a scientific panel, meeting in Washington, D.C., January 14, 15, and 16, 1953, to consider the problem of "flying saucers". The CIA-sponsored meeting is being held subsequent to a meeting of CIA, ATIC, and our representatives held at ATIC on December 12, 1952. At the December 12 meeting our representatives strongly recommended that a scientific panel not be set up until the results of our analysis of the sighting-reports collected by ATIC were available. Since a meeting of the panel is now definitely scheduled we feel that agreement between Project Stork and ATIC should be reached as to what can and what cannot be discussed at the meeting in Washington on January 14-16 concerning our preliminary recommendation to ATIC.

Experience to date on our study of unidentified flying objects shows that there is a distinct lack of reliable data with which to work. Even the best-documented reports are frequently lacking in critical information that makes it impossible to arrive at a possible identification, i.e. even in a well-documented report there is always an element of doubt about the data, either because the observer had no means of getting the required data, or was not prepared to utilize the means at his disposal. Therefore, we recommend that a controlled experiment be set up by which reliable physical data can be obtained. A tentative preliminary plan by which the experiment could be designed and carried out is discussed in the following paragraphs.

Based on our experience so far, it is expected that certain conclusions will be reached as a result of our analysis which will make obvious the need for an effort to obtain reliable data from competent observers using the [... unreadable...] necessary equipment. Until more reliable data are available, no positive answers to the problem will be possible.

Mr. Miles E. Coll -2- January 9, 1953
We expect that our analysis will show that certain areas in the United States have had an abnormally high number of reported incidents of unidentified flying objects. Assuming that, from our analysis, several definite areas productive of reports can be selected, we recommend that one or two of these areas be set up as experimental areas. This area, or areas, should have observation posts with complete visual skywatch, with radar and photographic coverage, plus all other instruments necessary or helpful in obtaining positive and reliable data on everything in the air over the area. A very complete record of the weather should also be kept during the time of the experiment. Coverage should be so complete that any object in the air could be tracked, and information as to its

altitude, velocity, size, shape, color, time of day, etc. could be recorded. All balloon releases or known balloon paths, aircraft flights, and flights of rockets in the test area should be known to those in charge of the experiment. Many different types of aerial activity should be secretly and purposefully scheduled within the area.

We recognize that this proposed experiment would amount to a large-scale military maneuver, or operation, and that it would require extensive preparation and fine coordination, plus maximum security. Although it would be a major operation, and expensive, there are many extra benefits to be derived besides the data on unidentified aerial objects.

The question of just what would be accomplished by the proposed experiment occurs. Just how could the problem of these unidentified objects be solved? From this test area, during the time of the experiment, it can be assumed that there would be a steady flow of reports from ordinary civilian observers, in addition to those by military or other official observers. It should be possible by such a controlled experiment to prove the identity of all objects reported, or to determine positively that there were objects present of unknown identity. Any hoaxes under a set-up such as this could almost certainly be exposed, perhaps not publicly, but at least to the military.

In addition, by having resulting data from the controlled experiment, reports for the last five years could be re-evaluated, in the light of similar but positive information. This should make possible reasonably certain conclusions concerning the importance of the problem of "flying saucers".

Results of an experiment such as described could assist the Air Force to determine how much attention to pay to future situations when, as in the past summer, there were thousands of sightings reported. In the future, then, the Air Force should be able to make positive statements, reassuring to the public, and to the effect that everything is well under control.
Very truly yours,

[unsigned]

H.C. Cross

NOTES:
1. VALLEE, Jacques. *Forbidden Science: Journals 1957-1969* (North Atlantic Books, 1992).

16. SO WHAT?

This chapter will annoy True Believers, and likely infuse True Skeptics with warm fuzzy feelings. I intend to provoke neither response—I'm not a True Believer *or* a True Skeptic. Those slots on the evolutionary chart represent extreme perspectives, and I'd like to think myself possessed of a more "balanced" sensibility, just as they do. No matter Colin Wilson's credo: "The Outsider's salvation lies in extremes." Not in *this* case.

The question has been asked: *So what if it's all real? UFOs, poltergeists, fortean events? What if some arm of government, or military intelligence,* does *have undeniable evidence of any of these? If publicly disclosed, would this reality lend relevance to day-to-day life? Improve our common lot?*

I think I can arguably claim *no.*

Put down that rock. I did say *arguably.*

If I can be said to "believe" anything, this would be that thing. The 21st century began not so well, and (if you accept media presentations) apparently is growing yet darker. Well, yes and no. As noted by Michael Crichton in his alarming—and bracing—*State of Fear* (2004) [1], much of our anxiety is media-generated. Crime statistics alone reasonably prove this, and if you've read the book you'll see this for yourself. If there exists a genuine conspiracy, it's that of media promotion of Dangerous World

Syndrome, where nothing, nowhere, and no one, is safe—ever. This mass deception is enhanced by advertising and politicians. *Protect Our Children! Safety First! Watch For Terrorists!*

I'm ashamed (not that much) that I can't remember where I first read the "Would proof of UFO/Paranormal events even be relevant in today's world?" statement. Compared to the potency of the very idea, its source doesn't matter overmuch. Why? When so many people believe the acronym *UFO* indicates *extraterrestrial vehicle*, I think my point is reasonably made. This shows a fundamental lack of critical thinking that reflects on a poor educational system, and America's seeming hostility toward both ideas and intellect. What can one deduce from a society that worships celebrities and athletes, yet refers to intelligent members as *geeks* and *nerds*? *And people* like *it that* way. What started this? In my teens, we called high achievers "smart" and athletes "jocks." I mean no insult to athletes, as I have been one myself. I'm sure you understand what I'm saying—at least I hope you do.

Sadly, most get news and information about the world only from TV and the Internet, both controlled by corporate money. And, since schools (including many colleges) rarely teach critical thinking, whatever the Expert of the Day proclaims is swallowed whole. "He's an *expert. I* don't know anything. His/her knowledge must be authentic."

Ufology—despite contrary claims from "insiders"—has no experts.

Nor does the field of paranormal investigation, though there are a handful of degreed people contributing exceptional work. George

P. Hansen, author of *The Trickster and the Paranormal* [2], certainly is high on that very short list. I cannot at present name another whose insight so staggers me, and recommend you seek out his book and articles.

"Funding for scientific investigation of the paranormal," notes Hansen, "has come almost entirely from wealthy individuals. Virtually no large philanthropic organizations or government bureaucracies have provided substantial, long-term support for the research. The only exceptions are the intelligence agencies—the only section of government formally allowed to use deception. Why does the money come from these sources?"

Hansen has spent eight years in parapsychology, working at both the Rhine Research Center in Durham, NC, and Psychophysical Research Laboratories in Princeton, NJ. He further informs us that "only two laboratories in the U.S. [are] devoted to parapsychology that employ two or more full-time scientists who publish in peer-reviewed scientific journals."

The state-of-the-art in ufology is much worse.

Hansen's writing—thankfully—is marked by controlled emotion and prose as tight as a time-lock. Casual readers might be challenged by explorations into liminality, anti-structure, and reflexivity. But the close effort is rewarded, as Hansen shows "a clear relationship between societal destructuring and the supernatural... Psi is irrational, but it is also real." He also stresses, perhaps above all, the ineffable power of the paranormal (and UFO encounters) to shatter human boundaries and status; how the phenomenon's deceptive nature puts it out of reach for those coming at it armed only with logic and rationality.

Hansen (along with Vallee and Keel) contributes ultimate intelligence to the problematic "so what?" posed by this chapter. So far as I'm concerned, he "proves" what the psychosocial school has been writing about for decades.

Lest I stand accused of hypocrisy in my apparent swallowing whatever the "experts" feed me, keep in mind that Vallee, Keel, and Hansen *have done the work.* Frankly, that very dedication and integrity probably had more than a little to do with John Keel's later ill health and death. These three (Vallee and Hansen still are involved with investigations; Vallee—by his own admission— behind the lines) were willing to hold their work up to whomever cared to cast a cold eye. Their encyclopedic knowledge, scrupulous documentation, journaling and personal stamina over decades is nothing short of astonishing.

The sum total of this all still might not ever accrue penultimate relevance, but does illuminate at least one genuine truth: The unexamined life is not worth living.

NOTES:
1. CRICHTON, Michael. *State of Fear* (Harper, 2004; reprint, 2009).
2. HANSEN, George. *The Trickster and the Paranormal* (Xlibris Corporation, 2001).

APPENDIX:

This end matter—a short story, an interview—is offered
because I feel it resonates with what has come before. "Broken
Symmetry" dramatizes what, to me, remains the most fascinating
(and confounding) aspect of many so-called entity sightings, with
or without UFO activity: the Interactive Effect. I refer mostly to
single-witness reports which, as noted by many writers before me,
are like having "no witness at all," due to an individual's subjective
perceptions and cultural bias; facts explored earlier in this book.
That realization alone is what prevents me from accepting a first-
level reading of UFOs and their alleged occupants as nuts-and-
bolts vehicles piloted by humanoid "aliens." Anyone reading this
should by now know that the phenomenon is stranger far than *that*
old Hollywood trope.

Publishing "Telegram from a Cold War Kid," a fairly long
interview with me conducted by Lee Munro of Otherworld North
East, might strike some readers as indulgent. Fair enough. But I
feel that Lee's intelligent approach evoked from me some less
formalized background information and, for those curious about a
writer's life, a glimpse into that marginal world.

BROKEN SYMMETRY

WILLIAM J. GRABOWSKI

"The underlying oneness in all confusions."
—Charles Hoy Fort
The Book of the Damned

Some people, I'm told, are lucky. They see things.

Gray Mercer, Rob Penfound, and Darcy Patel saw—

Never mind; we'll get there.

And lucky? I don't know. You'd have to ask them.

I did.

But I'm not lucky.

***

PHILLIP BOWLES: Thursday, November seventeenth, two thousand thirteen. Phil Bowles and Jim Neff here for BNI, interviewing Mr. Gray Mercer, fifty-seven, in his home, regarding his experience in West Edge Park on Monday, November fourteenth at approximately two ayem.

Mr. Mercer, please tell us what took place.

GRAY MERCER: [*Clears throat*] Sure. I'll try.

PB: Take as much time as you need.

GM: Thanks. I appreciate that—still feeling a little shaky.

PB: You sound better than earlier, during the pre-interview.

GM: Hmm...debatable. Glad you think so. Oh boy.

Had a late night, was walking home from work—programming for CyberSun Biotech—and passing a maintenance shed in the park. An odd feeling hit me [*shakes head*]. Hard to describe, but I'd compare it to anxiety, like expecting something.

PB: Expecting what?

GM: Can't say. The park is pretty much safe even at that hour. I've never in ten years had any trouble there. Never been afraid to cut through after work. Sorry to be so vague. In a nutshell, I felt *watched.*

PB: Watched. Would you expand that for us?

GM: Okay. Jeez, didn't think this would be so difficult. Uh— yeah. The sensation was akin to that of having a stranger glare at you for no apparent reason.

PB: Okay.

GM: Yeah. So I stopped, glanced around and listened. An odor in the air—something burning...real nasty, like roasting wire or plastic. Thought it might be coming from the shed.

PB: Had you ever smelled this odor in the park?

GM: No. Concerned me, though, so I moved closer to the shed, looking for smoke, any sign of fire. Quite a powerful reek. Stopping at the rear wall, I heard something humming and stepped around to the door. That's when I...when [*sighs*].

JAMES NEFF: It's okay. Take as long as you need, Gray.

GM: Thanks. I mean that. Don't like thinking about it. But I *saw.* Wasn't tired or stressed-out, either. In fact, except for the weird sensation, I felt pretty good.

JN: What did you see?

GM: What I saw, well. Something stood on the shed roof. Tall. Broad—much more so than a man. I just stood there with my mouth hanging open, thinking no, no, no. The thing might've been eight, maybe nine, feet tall. In the dark...I don't know. Hard to be sure, but certainly it was much larger than any man could be. I froze. Frankly, I was scared so bad I cried out [*gazes at ceiling*]. Anyone would've, seeing that. Oh God.

PB: Are you all right?

JN: Gray?

PB: We can break if—

GM: No. I mean yes, I'm okay. Best to get this out now. [*Long pause*] All right, I know I'm not troubled, or mentally ill. My position requires a twice-yearly psychological/physical evaluation. CyberSun's a government contractor.

JN: Understood, and noted.

GM: Thanks. The confidentiality of this is vital.

JN: And we'll abide that.

GM: Okay. What I saw was an awful thing. Just...awful.

I've never hallucinated, never used drugs, and I rarely drink. This thing saw me. And its eyes—looked like eyes, anyway— glowed like molten metal. Orange, with a blue tint. Orange, mostly. That was all too clear. Yeah. Can't rip it out of my mind— my dreams. Christ.

Something on its back. Hate to say it, but I think they were wings. Never felt such terror. Like you'd explode. I couldn't move.

PB: The entity. What was it doing?

GM: Nothing. Just standing there, glaring down at me like it was waiting, or testing my nerves. In that case I failed. Got dizzy and suddenly nauseated, with roaring in my ears. I wondered whether someone was messing with me. Prayed for this, actually. For some demented kid, one of those horror movie special-effects geeks.

Anything...anything but that fucking monster. Man, I need a glass of water.

PB: Absolutely. Let's break.

***

GM: Since that night I haven't been well. My doctor says I'm showing symptoms of malnutrition and—get this—evidence of radiation exposure. Can't see how either of those is even remotely possible. Radiation! And my diet is healthier than that of most of my friends. The radiation-thing scares the shit out of me. That's *nuts.* How could...[*shakes head*].

PB: We're going to help you with that.

GM: [*Weeping*] Oh God, oh God...thank you. I just wanna be done with this.

JN: We're absolutely here for you.

GM: I sure hope so. My work—they can't help. You know that.

PB: Yes.

GM: [*Whispering*] It spoke to me. In my head. My *mind.*

PB: It spoke. What did it say? What did it sound like?

GM: You two are very thorough, I'll give you that. I hope this interview is a one-time thing.

JN: It's okay.

GM: No, it's—

JN: We can stop.

GM: No! It said to me: "I saw your son." The goddamned thing said that, and in my mind it sounded like a drowning dog. Crazy. But that's what I heard. Jesus Christ! How did it know? *How?* Oh God, Jerry. My Jerry....

PB: I think we should stop, Gray.

GM: No. No. I want an *answer.* There must be a way to find out how—why it said that. Tell me. Please.

PB: Gray, look, you—

GM: I won't. Let me go on.

PB: [*Guardedly*] All right. You look very tired.

GM: Now *there's* an understatement. First my wife, then my son. She took off. Two years later, Jerry died. Or, rather, *was killed.* The right way to put it. That asshole Boy Scout activity leader got the urge for some rack-time with the girlfriend, abandoning his troops. They found Jerry, later, broken at the bottom of a ravine—animals had been at him.

Ever wanted to kill a man? I mean really do it?

PB: I'm so sorry, Gray. What a terrible thing. We ought to stop for today, pick up later if you care to. Don't you agree?

GM: I do not. Let's finish this.

PB: Your call. We know how hard this must be.

GM: You don't, sir. We'll leave it at that. Can't help my feelings.

I keep telling myself there must be a reason this happened to me, seeing whatever-it-was; hearing what it said. I'd give anything, do anything, to know *why*. I'll die trying. How does it know such things? What is it? Why does it exist?

PB: No one knows. All we have are theories, ways to talk about it.

JN: But we're here to bear witness and help as much as possible. We don't have all the answers. No one likes to think about these things, but the worst part is being alone with it—and you're no longer alone.

GM: Yeah. I understand.

PB: Others have had similar encounters. Did you know that?

GM: Yeah. Some local kids.

PB: They're trustworthy, too. We spoke with them, but you stood much, much closer to the entity. You're one of the very few.

GM: Lucky me.

***

It did not know what it was, where it came from, or why it existed.

But it knew everything about the others.

Where they lived; what they did; what they thought.

And their fears.

These drove them, more than anything in their lives of patterned, organized dullness. When they encountered it they came apart, terror seizing both mind and fragile flesh—consuming them.

When this happened, it saw everything.

Their dread. Lies. Illusions.

Love; what they feared losing. How profound this fear! That they bore it and lived still....

To some, very few, it spoke. In this it had no choice.

And in the night, still nothing could be secret. There existed no barrier it could not penetrate with the swarming charge behind its eyes. The devices with which the others communicated were as open and transparent as the very walls that sheltered them; as defenseless against manipulation as their frenzied minds.

How they suffered.

It could soar the poisoned sky, sink into pungent black earth where lay their dead, solemn and rotting.

It did what it did. Would continue until whatever drove it ended.

Then, perhaps, it might understand.

***

I switched off the recorder. Gray Mercer fixed me with a cold stare. "Sure wish I *felt* lucky, Phil."

Jim eyed Mercer as if anticipating violence.

Mercer, I knew, would not act out. After a decade in the "business," we knew how to read an interviewee; eyes, face, body language and posture often signified more than words could carry. Jim was overly tired, wary of his perceptions. You had to be careful. But I saw Mercer as sad, confused, and afraid—far more tired than Jim.

I said, "Gray, have you read any books about the paranormal? Anything on the Internet?"

He squinted, drew a deep breath. "Never. Nor would I. You can't believe that crap."

"But you saw something you can't explain, you—"

Jim shot me a glance: *Back off.*

Mercer clenched his teeth and stood. "Enough of this."

He looked as if he might collapse. "Gray," I said, "how about we go grab some food?"

He paused, sat, face pinched with whatever roiled behind it. "Food. I don't know. Might be a good idea."

He gave a forlorn smile. "C'mon," I said, "I'm buying—what do you think?"

Mercer nodded. "Okay."

Hearing this Jim visibly relaxed.

Mercer headed for the stairs, stopped short, and regarded me with eyes shiny and red. "Just need to wash my face."

Jim stood. "Great. You like Mexican?"

"More than I can say."

***

As we finished our chorizo and steaming tortilla soup, my cell phone chirped. I excused myself, stepped into the coat-check nook and took the call.

There had been another sighting.

A private investigator, this time.

Immediately I got back to the table, told Jim the news.

Mercer blotted his mouth with a napkin. "Hey," he said, "maybe I'm not crazy after all."

"You're not," Jim said. "Me and Phil are, though."

Mercer laughed.

Good. I feared treating him rudely so offered to interview the subject myself, but Mercer and Jim had finished eating and voiced no objection to leaving.

***

We drove Mercer home. I hoped my impatience didn't show. At the office I grabbed extra batteries for our gear, miffed that this small—and vital—detail had been overlooked. Not even one second could be wasted. Witnesses must be interviewed as soon as possible. Memory can be treacherous; particularly when there is trauma.

***

Private detective Rob Penfound, 43, proved to be another good witness.

We met him at his spacious loft on Burke Street, a home clearly arranged by a minimalist sensibility: racks of free weights; narrow kitchen bright with good-quality knives and cookware. Some may have found the place lacking in warmth, but in me it evoked a Zen-like calm.

We were offered coffee, for which I was grateful. Jim had faint purple patches under his eyes, and our heavy lunch must have been dragging him down.

Penfound sat on the edge of a black futon, no-nonsense posture as disciplined as his military-cut hair. The kind of guy who usually intimidates me. Not this afternoon, though.

Penfound's soul—and his fear—shone in his eyes.

He said, "I read in the *Daily Register* about the sightings. Man. Had myself a good laugh—you know, 'What the hell, people!' I'm a real skeptic. Spooky stories make me cringe. Not anymore."

"Tell us what happened," Jim said.

The other nodded, sipped bottled water. "Can't believe I'm doing this. Got your number from the local police—*great* conversation, there.

"I was working a potential divorce case, surveilling a woman—for once—whose husband suspected her of extracurricular activity. Well, guys, he was correct. Am I offending you?"

"Not at all," Jim said, "life happens."

Penfound chuckled. "That it does. Anyway, I followed the wife to Proxy's—that hell-hole next to Luciano's Pizza—where she hooked up with a man waiting in the lot. They embraced."

"Her lover," I said.

"Can't make that assumption. Could be her brother, a close friend, you can't tell. Sounds like bullshit, I know, but it's true. Mistakes have been made. But this one turned out to be the real thing."

I felt sluggish. "Sorry, Rob. Jumping the gun. We appreciate your being efficient. Facts are what we need."

"Not a problem. Okay. After dark they left the bar, drove in his car to the Blue Pool Motel, and did what people do there. Like minks. I used a parabolic microphone."

Jim clunked his mug onto Penfound's teak coffee table. Penfound gazed at the table. "You familiar with the parabolic mike?"

Jim and I nodded, knew the device—a small dish-like "gun" with a grip and projecting rod—is capable of detecting and amplifying sound from wherever it is aimed. It can "hear" even through walls.

"They were going at it," Penfound went on, "so I had what I needed to establish a case, when an extremely loud shriek came through—popped my headset. Good thing, because my eardrums would've ruptured. Just incredibly loud. Even my teeth ached."

Jim scribbled in his notebook. "Were you injured?"

"Nah. Set me back a good thousand bucks, though." He drank the last of his water. "Refills?"

We both needed one and said so.

Penfound switched to an energy-drink. "A couple seconds after the shriek, I saw a flash above the motel. Lightning, I thought, not realizing how rare that is in November. Weird. It *hung* in the sky for five, six seconds...then vanished. Poof. Don't have to explain to you guys how sensitive the P-mike is. Thought I'd caught a lightning-blast. Wrong."

Penfound squinted, replaying the encounter in his mind. Jim said, "Were there any odors?"

"No. Wait. There was something, which I thought was the fried circuitry in my P-mike. Probably *was* that."

He was stalling.

The unknown stood in shadow behind his ordered life, and Rob Penfound fought against rising fright.

Softly, he said, "Then the real fun started. At first I thought I was having a seizure...just like my father used to. Flashing lights could bring one on, but I have no history. I'll tell you, this fear came. Totally goddamned inappropriate—and I saw a tall, bulky shape standing at the motel's south end.

"Really rattled me, but even so could've been some big-ass drunk taking a leak. That's what I told myself."

Penfound shook his head and stood, stepped across the room and plucked something from atop a bookcase. On his way back he gazed at whatever it was he held. "What I saw," he said, "looked kind of like this."

Penfound handed the object to me. "Just imagine one," he went on, "with no neck or ears and about nine feet tall."

"Let me see," Jim said.

I passed it over, and he scrutinized the thing as if it might be priceless. "Hmm...an owl, huh?"

***

It liked the broken, worn-out places; vacant buildings and their silent desolation. The abandoned.

Such spaces rang vivid and true, mirroring the misery, the secrets, of those who once occupied them. The watched.

And those who had ended.

The ended. Lost, raging and afraid, lingered still. Across ages of gnawing vigilance, it recognized them as earthbound wraiths. Prisoners of untold cravings, of guilt and indulgence.

How they howled their terror; their lacerating ruin.

It manifested before them, and they feared its scrutiny. Some, little more than swarming debris, flocked to it as if an end to suffering. A hand to feed hungers blacker far than outermost space.

Those who could manage spoke nonsense: *Help me, God...Gabriel...Satan...Mother... Father....*

Hailing and blunt, the words sank like stones into oblivion.

Pattern-less among pattern-makers, it gathered only chaos. Waves, convections, pulses. Even this proved difficult.

But it was learning.

***

I recalled what Gray Mercer had said about his sighting in the park. "An owl," I said.

Rob Penfound took the white porcelain figure, returned it to its perch atop the bookcase. "If I knew of a better example, I'd give one."

I said, "Rob, how far were you from what you saw?"

"Forty, fifty feet. Close enough..."

"It was dark, I know, but could you see a face?"

Abruptly he glared at me. "Hey! What I really want to know, guys, can you tell me if this thing is real? Can it be touched?"

Jim nodded. "It's real. What it might be we don't know—we're trying to determine that. Spend the better part of our lives running around at all hours. Wouldn't have it any other way."

Penfound gave a grim smile. "Amen to that, brother. You said it's real...well, what do you *think* it might be?"

I swallowed hard, drew a deep breath and sighed. "Our investigations and research point toward a nonhuman intelligence, one capable of assuming physical form—however temporary that may be. And more. These entities are tricksters. People see different things."

Penfound sipped from his Red Bull. "How can that be?"

"We're not sure...perhaps something to do with the witnesses' ethnicity, religious beliefs—or their absence. It's amazingly complex and disturbing, with very few reputable scientists willing to investigate, put themselves on the line."

Penfound's hard face assumed a pensive cast, like someone afraid to admit he's lost. "Well, that sounds like something beyond my control. Goddamn..."

"Please continue," Jim said.

"All right. It moved, kind of awkwardly, toward my car. *Big* goddamned thing. And the closer it got, the more I pushed back against my seat—like *that* would help! Christ. It stopped. White, pure white. First time I saw, don't know why, I thought it looked grayish, ashy.

"It turned and looked at me. The fright hit like a punch. The eyes were...like bicycle reflectors, hypnotic, maybe two inches in diameter. Felt like I was five years old again, about to piss myself."

"Others report the same sensation," Jim said. "You're not alone there."

"It faced me. When it did that, I felt like the only person alive...a terrible sort of...*loneliness.* Don't know how else to describe it."

"Tell us everything, no matter how trivial it may seem."

"None of it seems trivial. I felt *vulnerable.* Not used to feeling that. One other thing. I thought of my father. Images...overwhelming—this crushing guilt."

Jim said, "These images, did they come naturally? Or as if from outside?"

"Struck a nerve, there. Outside...like a broadcast. Creepy as shit, man. I hated it. Complete loss of control. I got the hell outta there, guys."

Jim nodded. "You've given us a lot, Rob. Anything you'd like to add?"

Penfound paused, gazed at the floor. "I wish I'd gotten to know my father better. Miss 'im like hell. That's what I'd like to add."

"Thank you. We might publish this interview. Okay if we use your name?"

Penfound stood. "Sure. Guess that's fine. I'm not ashamed."

I shook his hand. "Thanks, Rob. You're adding solid credibility to the entire matter. I admire your bravery."

He was going to need that bravery.

Most witnesses to the unknown have no idea how risky it is to go public.

We promised to follow up in a few weeks. Some people have but one experience with the phenomenon; others, many. There can be no predicting the effect on their lives.

One thing we *did* know: whatever the ultimate source of these anomalies—"monsters," UFOs, ghosts, mysterious "people" like the so-called men-in-black—theirs is an inhuman intelligence, seemingly hostile or perhaps indifferent to ours; strangely fractured. We may never understand it.

In my bleaker moments I wonder why we bother.

***

The next two weeks flogged us. Worse, my wife came down with some flu-like illness that flattened her for six days. Tending to Diane, I read through the transcripts from our various interviews.

Our town and its more rural neighbors were besieged by

anomalous events. So many, there was no way for Bowles Neff Investigation to cover even one-third of these. Indeed, the entire region was undergoing a "wave" of UFO and monster-sightings. Waves occur once or twice every ten years, as they did in 1947, 1952, 1966, 1973, 1984, etc. No one knows why, but serious investigators theorize something akin to a conditioning pattern that combines periodicity with unpredictability. We do not understand the motivations (if indeed there are any) behind this, nor who or what is responsible. But the implications are ominous—even chilling. Ignoring the phenomenon or pretending it does not exist, is irresponsible and, quite possibly, dangerous.

The best we can do is track and document the sightings. Observe the effects on witnesses and treat them with the human decency others may be denying them.

We're watching the Watchers.

***

Wednesday, I was about to call Gray Mercer when Jim dashed into the office. "Drop whatever you're doing, we've got a sighting in progress!"

Not Jim's usual laid-back style—he couldn't be joking. I stood. "What kind? Where?"

"Entity. Cross Falls—some picnic area near the ballpark." He clamped his cell phone to his ear. "Yeah—ten minutes. Of course. Stay put."

Already he trotted down the hall toward the parking lot. I grabbed my keys and followed.

***

In the truck Jim prepped our cameras and recorders. "A Darcy Patel," he said, "is seated at a picnic table on her lunch break. I had a hard time hearing, for obvious reasons, but she says the entity is about thirty feet up a pine tree, apparently unaware of her."

I had the truck pushing sixty, my heart hammering. "Can't believe it."

"Christ, I know. Hope she's able to sit still."

"Don't count on it."

"Oh *man.*" Jim grinned, nodded.

"Look out for traffic," I warned, "and cops—we're way over."

"You got it."

We barreled out of town, and I held back when the needle ticked eighty.

The road dipped, walled by dark spiky pines. One or two minutes passed—almost there.

"On the right—watch it," Jim said.

"I see them."

Two girls on mountain bikes crossed the road.

Here was the picnic area.

Nosing the truck into a parking slot, I killed the engine and we climbed out. Careful not to slam the door, Jim plucked our gear from the seat and we made for the trail Darcy Patel had described over her cell phone.

The unseasonably warm weather had worked in our favor, bringing Ms. Patel out for what she'd hoped a quiet lunch.

Moving as stealthily as possible, after a hundred feet or so, we came to a small clearing, air rich with pine dust—and more.

Jim glanced at me, pointed at his nose.

An odor, like burning wire, stood out in that silent space. I fought to control my gushing breath.

Darcy Patel, head tilted back, sat still and solemn as the forest.

Hearing us, she glanced over her shoulder grinning, eyes wide and brown.

"Oh," Jim whispered, "oh my God..."

He aimed the camera and started shooting, sweat beading his brow.

Darcy again looked our way, and I could see she wept, mouth opening and closing as if fighting for air.

Suddenly Jim cried out—collapsed in a gasping sprawl.

At that moment a moaning gale swayed the pines, bearing our future for good or ill.

***

In St. Luke's emergency room I had a hard time explaining our situation. The attending physician (a pale man with tiny round glasses who looked barely of drinking-age) regarded me with a quizzical squint. Had trouble with the words *paranormal, anomalous phenomena* and, especially, *entity.*

So unimaginative, these youngsters. I'll tell you, doctor or no, I wanted to deck the guy.

Darcy Patel, a complete stranger, kept repeating, "Please let him be okay...please let him be okay."

I echoed this mantra.

The doctor—Reisner or Riser?—asked whether Mr. Neff used recreational drugs. Dammit, hadn't he asked Jim?

An hour later Doctor R. reported that Mr. Neff had fainted from low blood-sugar and some kind of shock. True, Jim hadn't eaten. True, he'd had a "shock," all right. But he passed all the vital tests and was released.

I can't help wondering how well the good doc might have held up, seeing what Jim had seen.

And I had not.

***

We gathered in my home: my wife, Jim and his girlfriend Tina, and Darcy Patel. After a hearty round of roast beef sandwiches and coffee, we settled a bit.

Darcy appeared happy, yet cried and cried. "I am so thrilled," she said. "I can hardly bear it. *Garuda.* We saw it—and so clearly. Unbelievable."

Seated across from her, I could see and hear the jolt of hysteria. Darcy's eyes shone with ecstasy and dread; her voice tight with a terrible yearning, perhaps years of it. (She'd told us of a bleak childhood orphaned in Calcutta, where both material and spiritual starvation were common.) She mustn't let the sighting implode her life into a kind of metaphysical anarchy. After all, we didn't even know what we were dealing with.

"Darcy," I said, "weren't you afraid?"

She pursed her lips. "Yes. Of course. Garuda is not beautiful, in the way we apprehend beauty. It is not meant to be. We are right to fear, because Garuda gazes into our souls."

She *does* understand, I told myself.

On my birthday (mere days before Gray Mercer's sighting) an old friend had brought from Tibet a distressing tale, and a carving depicting the fierce, winged Garuda carrying Vishnu the Protector to blood and glory. The synchronicity of the gift chills me still.

I said, "These entities have ruined many lives—people have died in connection with them—"

"Oh," Darcy said. "No...those who die are the craven, the self-indulgent. Their own fear helps to kill them, like cancer of the soul."

"In that case," Jim muttered, "we're all doomed."

"Jim!" Tina said.

Had I heard correctly?

Jim's pale face and ugly grimace failed to hide his anger, his fear.

***

Some people are lucky.

They see things.

Gray Mercer...Rob Penfound...Darcy Patel.

Jim Neff.

They saw, and you—reading this—know they did. You don't know *what* they saw.

Nor do I.

Because I saw nothing.

I have never *seen.*

Even after gazing for hours and hours at the photos Jim managed to take. Weeping over them. I've tried fooling myself:

Your vision is shot, pal. Nothing. Perhaps some day I'll be strong enough to admit that to Diane, Jim, and all the others. Perhaps not.

Ruin takes many forms. Some of us suffer because we aren't allowed to glimpse the unknown and its terrible truth...its deceptive beauty.

Sometimes I wonder if I'm the lucky one.

Over and over, I choke on the grim fact: There is no fool worse than a sentimental one. How to admit my soul is an empty room, waiting for the unknown to enter. To have the symmetry of day and night broken.

Waiting.

Watching.

150

TELEGRAM FROM A COLD WAR KID:
AN INTERVIEW WITH WILLIAM J. GRABOWSKI
Conducted by Lee Munro of Otherworld North East

LEE MUNRO: Quick intro question Bill: which book-title most aptly reflects your mood today?

GRABOWSKI: At this moment—12:38 AM—that would have to be Ted Holiday's *The Goblin Universe*. Why? Because in proofing my forthcoming book, *Black Light*, I realized that no matter what I've set down there, my gut tells me nothing can be more haunted than human beings. The book's subtext more or less tells readers how, and why, I reached that view...not *conclusion*, because I don't really accept "final" knowledge. Anything involving human activity is forever uncertain.

Holiday decided not to publish his disturbing, well-reasoned study, and after Holiday's death Colin Wilson (whom I interviewed in 1986 for *The Gate*) got permission from Ted's family to put out *The Goblin Universe*. The book explored so-called cryptids—i.e., Nessie and others—in a way not done before and shorn of personal belief. This ended badly for the author. Here was a guy making connections between slippery (no pun there) sightings, and the far more troubling possibility that human consciousness might indeed have a hand in such matters. As you probably know, Holiday died very near where he'd once had what can be described as a "man-in-black" experience. He'd been glared at for no good reason by a silent, menacing guy wearing motorcycle leathers. A heart-attack ended him literally on the spot of that sighting.

I hate such accounts, but they exist. The "underground," or taboo topics, in an already fringed-out field. Personally, I think he was so freaked out by what he discovered, that he feared even discussing it—hence the no-publish decision on *Goblin Universe*. True to the end, though, he had the presence of mind and steely will to record the incident...very different from the "usual" MIB accounts.

MUNRO: **As a working writer I imagine you need to wear two hats: a business hat, and a creative hat. I'm interested— how does one approach inform the other? Also when, say, you ghost-write something, is your "creative ego" put out by not getting recognized for creating (if that makes sense!)?**

GRABOWSKI: Glad you asked, Lee. It's tough having a foot in each world, and keeping body and soul together. It's often brutal, with sleep-deprivation and all its wonderful health effects. Not too far off topic, here's an aside: having worked my share of suit-and-tie jobs in the 1990s, experiencing corporate America just on the cusp of the Internet, I saw brilliant engineers reduced to clinical alcoholism and tears over some project manager's hang-ups with company promotion. Quote: "We can't have this jerk-off geek pictured on our brochures." Well, several of those geeks moved on to California and Silicon Valley—and taught me the fine art of balancing business practicalities with creative endeavors.

Though it might—in our current global culture of people too busy to live—be a cliché, my old pals showed me that no one cares how much you know, until they know how much you care. Despite the occasional ego-burst, I've never forgotten that. The lesson has guided me, in meeting with witnesses to the unknown, never to deny them the common reality of human emotion—of the hauntedness of being born into a world brimming with war and strife and mystery. We're not as smart as we think—cleverness is not ethical intellect.

Now...back to your question! I delegate about 30% of my work-day to writing and submitting proposals, responding to project invites from prospective (and repeat) clients requiring various writerly services. You're right to bring up the "creative ego" aspect of ghostwriting, as it *is* often painful to remain anonymous in the wake of sweating blood over six weeks—or whatever—spent researching and hammering out a thriller, or what have you, employing one's best fictive "magic."

Simply put, ghostwriting gives me the financial freedom to pursue projects that would be impossible to write if I had to constantly stress out over paying bills. It can be exhausting, and I carefully structure a set amount of hours each day to such work. Newer (hell, *all*) writers need to really, really *want* to work hard in our current hostile, anti-intellectual world...and be savvy as hell in learning the art of selling their wares. Social media makes this easier, but is more demanding than in the old days of typewriters and snail-mail. For some arcane reason, clients expect a 24/7 presence. I average about 10,000 words per week keeping up, leaving not much time for my own projects—and sleep!

MUNRO: If you were giving a class on writing, which books or articles would top your essential reading list?

GRABOWSKI: Right away, there is no better guide than William Strunk, Jr. and E.B. White's *The Elements of Style*. A 92-page bible of what to do—and what to avoid. I've worn out over the decades five copies of this little paperback. My favorite of their advice: "Omit needless words." *Hell* yes, brother—I'm all for that! England's own Lynn Truss's *Eats, Shoots & Leaves* has also proved an amazingly valuable—and funny—tool I constantly refer to.

MUNRO: Much of your fiction-writing seems to have paranormal/Fortean/just-plain-weird overtones, or as Jim Morrison might have put it, something "not quite at-home." Are you drawn to these themes because, as a writer, they allow you to explore a particular essence of storytelling, or are you drawn because of your interest in these topics *away* from writing?

GRABOWSKI: Cool as all get-out you mention Jim Morrison —a big influence. Mostly on following your "personal" muse no matter where she takes you. What a gifted, tormented, sadly self-destructive soul he was…America's Arthur Rimbaud. It's easy to overlook how young he was—how brief his candle burned. That *voice!* Those lyrics, stabbing your soul like a doomed prophet…. His "betters" treated him like shit, and long may they roast along with drug dealers who exploited his sensitivity and chronic fear of nothingness—of crying into a war-filled void vicious and hungry for his next screaming wake-up call, heedless of the cost. His presence haunts me, because he was the first—along with your country's unmatched Black Sabbath, Pink Floyd, Hawkwind and a few others—to embrace everything beautiful and mad and strange about simply being alive in a fragmented world.

Man, that was a bit of a long response, eh? In my own fictive works, I wholly embrace the fabulously "weird" ideas of Charles Fort, John Keel, Jacques Vallee, and more obscure writers like François Rabelais, Djuna Barnes, Andre ("father" of Surrealism) Breton, Celine, Yeats, and that teetotaler Dylan Thomas. Plus a few present-day visionaries like the late, extremely lamented Michael McDowell, Thomas Ligotti, Joyce Carol Oates, Caitlín R. Kiernan, Peter Straub, T.E.D. Klein and several others. Not only for visionary ideas, but for sheer compression of thought. Every writer ought to read poetry, because it teaches how to render both ferocious emotion and sensual delights—and torture. I often wonder what the old surrealists might make of our jittery, attention-challenged global culture, where a guy in Germany can instantly respond to my Twitter reckonings on how best to grow habanero chiles!

I'm drawn to constant pursuit of life's sheer strangeness—to Jean Cocteau's wondering why we don't simply dissolve in our bath-water. I guess I would call this an interest—nay, obsession—with why we're here at all, and what it's worth. I suppose this is why so much of my fiction explores "monsters" and what they teach us about the most fierce, despairing and searching, aspects of our enigmatic lives.

MUNRO: **I first became aware of your work after stumbling across your Night Run blog, which I guess chronicles some of your writing and thoughts during the process of composing your book *BLACK LIGHT: Perspectives on Mysterious Phenomena*, which will be published this year. Can you give a background to the book, and what your aim was in writing it?**

GRABOWSKI: *Black Light* is my summation—no sequels—of all things uncanny and/or troubling I've experienced that seem to have no logical explanation, so will not have much in common with straight-out books exploring UFOs and other so-called paranormal phenomena. Who wants that? Sure, there will always be an audience for the next Roswell (non)explanation—myself seated front-row. Otherworld's interview with the amazingly prolific Nick Redfern showed me the folly of "closure" on all things paranormal, a term I have trouble with. Nick might (my opinion only) agree that what we call "paranormal" is simply what we label undiscovered science. Or maybe not.

Science *does not* (at least not yet) have all the answers, and is way too reckless in dismissing alternate opinions. Seriously, Lee. I might step outside right now (in West Virginia, 25 miles from where the so-called Sistersville airship sightings of 1897 were reported; and 75 miles from Woodrow Derenberger's so-called Indrid Cold meeting) and bear witness to…what? A meandering Keelian light? A winged monstrosity with terrible red-glowing eyes? Here's the thing. Would I dare tell anyone–even you—if I did? I would instantly—perhaps foolishly—approach the "anomaly." I'd worry about my mental health; my misperceiving a barn owl—scary damned things, let me tell you. Above all, *Black Light* is a chronicle of a searcher, one wary of the paranormal, but haunted by early experience with the unknown. Chapter One does its best to play fair with the reader in recalling what might have been an authentic encounter with what Carl Jung termed a "psychically overwhelming Other." Frankly, I don't know *what* I saw, but know enough not to confuse ill-recalled dream imagery with some physical creature outside my 10-year-old's experience. Memory is tricky, and I hadn't given the incident a single second's thought until first reading John Keel's *Mothman Prophecies*, where he tells of witnesses in nearby northwest Pennsylvania encountering bizarre (yet organic-seeming) "birds" moving between rows of corn—and the memory of my encounter punched me like a fist. These unknowns were described as being nearly eight-feet-tall, with straight pointed beaks. The "bird" I saw was nowhere near that tall, a black-eyed "penguin" perhaps two-feet tall, with a straight beak. It scared the hell out of me, and I took a few bee-stings standing watching it—my long-gone mother thought some pervert had gotten hold of me. The entire incident, I know, rings of boyish bullshit—but there you go. A rare daylight experience.

I was not aware that Ohio was undergoing a UFO "wave" in 1968, nor that a policeman that same year (Dale Spauer) had chased a saucer up to the border of Pennsylvania—and had his life ruined. Worse, he took refuge in the Solon Motel—in my home town. I knew none of this until much later in life. I admit this might be a case of connecting unrelated events—but it remains to me suspicious. A sort of resonance. The incident sparked my becoming a writer, and my fascination with the unknown. I couldn't have known that John Keel himself investigated the Spauer incident, which I read about much later in his ominous *The Eighth Tower.* It's listed under Ravenna, Ohio—where Officer Spauer began his car-chase.

MUNRO: You've recently had a post published on the Magonia Blog regarding John Keel's *The Mothman Prophecies*, and how it affected and influenced you. More than that, however, you've had feet on the ground in Point Pleasant, talking to people and scratching behind the myth. Maybe a big question, but peeking behind the curtain of common perception, what's your take on the Mothman events, and how the town and its people have been affected by it—either by the events in the story, or the attention brought on by them?

GRABOWSKI: What a well-timed question, Lee! I have explored Point Pleasant and the TNT area at length. Boy have I! Everything short of raking the soil—like *that* would do any good. Up front, let me say I do know the difference between fascination and obsession—or do I? In my mind, all I've carried out in Point Pleasant is both. How could it be otherwise? I ask you, how can any seeker of the unknown *not* be taken with visiting a site so (in)famous? And less than four hours from home? Man.

My "take" is only a few degrees different from much previously written about all things Mothman/UFOs/MIB and other deep weirdness. My forthcoming book, though, delves deeper into the matter. I hung out with older residents...asked some damned personal questions I'm lucky didn't get my ass kicked, and recorded all I heard. I was astounded by the responses. You probably know of the annual Mothman Festival (created by the incredibly hard-working Jeff Wamsley), active since 2003 in Point Pleasant, WV. The biggest mistake made by cynical cable-TV documentaries (not all, but most) is in assuming the friendly residents are drunken rednecks—what a goddamned insult. Far from the reality of sharing meals with those who lost loved ones when the Silver Bridge fell on 15 December 1967—13 months to the day of the first major Mothman sighting. I choose not to delve into numerological synchronicity—what would that prove?

I found locals divided: those who resent the festival, and those who embrace it. The very few folks I met who claimed to have witnessed UFOs are still shaken, but more so by the MIB "visits." What you won't read in any other book is that Point Pleasant grew used to the seemingly "scheduled" overflights of aerial machines bright with prismatic lighting—described to me as "diamond pure." Keel himself had that experience, witnessing a green-lit saucer hovering over a lonely hill I have personally visited—for what that's worth. Keel was no bullshitter—my opinion. He never once exploited any witness, and made less than $5,000 from publication of *The Mothman Prophecies*—until this was decades later remedied by the movie-makers. Despite what you might think you know about John Keel, he was frightened by what he found. A farmhouse puppy whose heart had been cut out in a perfect circle. Telephone messages warning against some horrible event— documented in Keel's personal letters between himself and local newspaper reporter Mary Hyre—set to occur on the Ohio River. Whoever phoned in this prophecy either caused the bridge-fall, or knew who was going to engineer it. No matter—in my opinion—that the bridge was in poor repair. Someone knew, and they dicked around with Keel, who warned Mary Hyre not to speak of it.

To me, this is far more disturbing than Mothman or UFOs, and speaks of industrial sabotage. The nearest (at that time) bridge was in Ravenswood, quite a distance from Point Pleasant. Keel never wrote about the MIB visiting insurance offices, where blueprints for local energy concerns were located. Andy Colvin has written much about about this. It explains the absurd behavior ("What is your time?") of so-called men-in-black, not to mention the well-dressed man Keel confronted in the TNT area at night, who was talking into a microphone and would only "grunt" at Keel's questions. This is very telling about human manipulation of what might have begun with authentic sightings of a cryptid. I've knocked around desolate buildings (especially the Lakin Industrial Home for Colored Boys across from the TNT area)—since demolished, and can testify to the utter eeriness of the region. Subjective? Of course—what isn't? And what do we make of the Point Pleasant branch of Defense Logistics Agency, recently shut down? Many red flags. Keel never went public with reports of gone-missing teens in Point Pleasant between 1966-1968. A taboo subject you'll be hard-pressed to find, even though it's been reported that remains were found in shallow caves in the TNT area. This invests the whole Mothman mystery with more than is commonly acknowledged. Thanks for hearing me out!

MUNRO: We've talked previously about some aspects of reported anomalous phenomena, and I know you at times have been drawn to, let's call it a Jungian perspective. Can you say something about how some of Jung's work might inform approaches to people's experiences?

GRABOWSKI: I can. While no one can be sure of its importance, Jung did point out—after thousands of sessions—the apparent continuum between dream imagery and waking life. How the unconscious guides us by way of a universe of symbols. Ideas as dismaying as any paranormal theories—including UFOs and "entities" like Mothman. We should be happy that Jung wrote a book about UFOs, though primarily considered them latent symbols of wholeness. This to me is an idea almost too scary to bear–that *we* create our gods and monsters and UFOs. Frankly, I think he hit the proverbial nail's head. Even a cursory review of Vallee's *Passport to Magonia* and its incredible list of sightings tells us that UFOs and even ghostly phenomena manifest in accordance with the given country's culture. Violent "monsters" in South America. Science Fiction absurdities in the USA (oddly aligned with UK sightings). Surreal beings whose clothing and vehicles, luminous blue and violet and green, speak absurd poetry in France, and ice-hacking dwarves in arctic regions, tell a very "anthropological" tale.

MUNRO: Are there other approaches, writers or thinkers who you think might inform, or at least generate, interesting thought experiments when it comes to anomalous experiences?

GRABOWSKI: After decades of thinking about these things,

and changing my mind to mostly accept the Magonian/Fortean psychosocial theory, I'm left alone in what feels like a very sophisticated joke, or test, inflicted upon random people. By "alone," I mean unpopular. Sure, I'd love nothing more than for 1950s-type helmet-headed ufonauts to be real—and to care about us! To take us away from daily stress and our awful awareness of Death's hound sniffing our souls. I'm neither arrogant nor ironic saying this, Lee. Simply amazed and afraid that I'm alive at all, and subject at any time to experience some localized, high-strangeness event...just like anyone. I find it easy to ignore the infantile believers in Grays, etc., but never enough to completely dismiss them. Think they're wrong and that I'm "right." Who knows? Not me. I am convinced, though, that we share our world with another intelligence—even one we might daily create—that is as strange as "God," and that's enough to keep me looking. Even if there are no UFOs or ghosts or entities external to us, isn't that absolutely mind-blowing that we *think* there are? That we don't really know who *we* are? Sometimes I think we get the gods we deserve.

MUNRO: During your time of interest in anomalous subjects, how have you seen the subjects or approaches to them change? Do you see a regression, as opposed to progression, in thinking or perception?

GRABOWSKI: What a great question! Ever since my uncle Joe gave me [George] Adamski's—poor bastard!—*Inside the Flying Saucers*, I've gone through believing in extraterrestrials visiting us in metal machines, "demonology," collective human despair (not done with that), right up to what I suppose is called the psychosocial theory. I'm 95% convinced we are actively engaged in creating our evolution—like playful children in charge of watercolors. That remaining 5% is important. Very. We don't know everything. Probably never will. The whole "unknown" business might very well be in charge—for good or ill. I do—at least in America, with some UK crossover—see a regrettable lapse into "alien abduction" and apocalyptic visions of powerlessness. Very scary stuff, with crossovers into political tyranny and nutty comfort cults. You can't be involved with this and not feel a bit paranoid— god knows I have my share. And the increasing erosion of individual liberties frightens me. We seem poised on living in a world worse than that envisioned in the *Terminator* movies, because human-controlled. The Internet is often as frightening as Skynet!

MUNRO: We're both dancers under the spell of the music that moves us. So, I want you to suggest some songs/artists; a soundtrack to a story you've written that stands out as a favorite, a soundtrack to accompany you while you sit in the dark in your favorite chair with the lights out holding a glass of your favorite tipple, and a soundtrack to walking around the abandoned TNT plant outside Point Pleasant at 3:33am.

GRABOWSKI: Now you've done it! Music is a huge presence —perhaps overly so—in my life. I've been a drummer in several Cleveland bands—years ago. My favorites are atmospheric stuff: Massive Attack, Tangerine Dream, Klaus Schulze, Low (whose "Half Light" graces the movie soundtrack of my pal Mark

Pellington's *The Mothman Prophecies*), Opeth, and thanks to England, King Crimson, Genesis (pre-1976, with Peter Gabriel), as well as REM, Nine Inch Nails, Skinny Puppy, Fear Factory, Ministry, and a lot of Tom Waits. And let's not forget Mozart and Wagner, those happy tricksters.

MUNRO: What do you have in the Grabowski pipeline? Any new fiction or non-fiction you're working on?

GRABOWSKI: I've been writing, behind all my other projects, a huge novel over the past 2 years, an attempt to convey the reactions of a small town to an enigmatic presence that seems like God. It's more complex and strange than it sounds. We'll see…

MUNRO: Thanks for your time, Bill. One more question. I know you're a big fan of cooking. So you've invited OWNE around to dine. What the hell—Keel, Vallee and Jung are turning up too (hey, it's my movie; I'll script it how I want!). What divine culinary experience would you prepare for us?

GRABOWSKI: I know that Keel (rest him well) and Vallee wouldn't mind beefy dishes. Same for Jung. I would hope you and OWNE give me warning of any vegetarians…I used to be one. In a perfect meeting, you would be served Chicken Vindaloo, Ghost-Chile Stew, and a sweet ice-box lemon pie. With absinthe.

LEE MUNRO, B.Sc (Hons) is an assistant clinical trial manager with a degree in psychology. His primary role and interest within the research team is methodology and experiment development, the psychology and development of belief, audio analysis and field survey.

ABOUT THE AUTHOR

Independent writer/editor William J. Grabowski is the author of 4 books and over 300 short stories, articles, interviews and reviews. Recent work (with John Kluge) is on the Web at Forbes, 2 Paragraphs, Magonia Blog, Hellnotes, Horror World; and in magazines *Cemetery Dance* and National Public Radio-associated *Wireless*, as well as in Daniel Howard's anthology of science fiction, fantasy, and horror, *Visions of Imagination*. Emmy Award-winning investigative journalist George Knapp lauded Grabowski's work on syndicated radio show *Coast to Coast AM*. A five-year stint as contributing editor with World Fantasy Award-winning *The Horror Show* earned him a nomination from SPWAO as best nonfiction writer. Currently he contributes articles several times per week to 2 Paragraphs.com, reviews books for UK print/eZine *Beware the Dark*, and is writing a new "epic" novel. He enjoys Punk, dark music, and hot chilies.

www.ingramcontent.com/pod-product-compliance
Lightning Source LLC
Chambersburg PA
CBHW050122280326
41933CB00010B/1209